"*Freely Sober* is an invitation to step into more awareness, honest exploration, and inner wrestling concerning your relationship with alcohol. Ericka Andersen has a special way of articulating the nuances Christians feel when it comes to drinking without using legalism, labels, or rules. The message of this book is one of freedom and hope!"

Jenn Kautsch, founder of the SoberSis Community and author of *Look Alive, Sis*

"Ericka Andersen has written one of the most important books for Christian women and drinking. It is kind, understanding, packed with not just knowledge but wisdom, and is the perfect resource for really anyone looking to change their relationship with alcohol. Whether you're hoping for big changes or small wins, this book and its thoughtful approach will help you. It's filled with thoughtful questions, helpful exercises, and practical advice from someone who has been exactly where you are . . . and still is. 10/10."

Jonathon M. Seidl, author of *Confessions of a Christian Alcoholic: A Candid Conversation on Drinking, Addiction, and How to Break Free*

"Ericka Andersen brings a rare brilliance to the complex conversation around alcohol and faith, offering Christian women compassionate, grounded guidance through what can feel like a maze of mixed messages and emotions. Her writing is refreshingly vulnerable, deeply researched, and full of practical insight. I highly recommend *Freely Sober* to anyone who has ever questioned whether alcohol is adding to—or quietly subtracting from—their life. This is a conversation you deserve to have."

Heather Harpham Kopp, author of *Sober Mercies: How Love Caught Up with a Christian Drunk*

"It is time for us to have this much-needed conversation, and who better to lead us on this delicate journey than Ericka Anderson? *Freely Sober* carries a vulnerable strength that can only come from the heart of one who has truly been delivered from the prison of addiction. Through telling parts of her own story while weaving honest and strategic reflection for the reader, Ericka is a trustworthy confidant for those looking for hope and desperate for freedom."

Natalie Runion, author of *Raised to Stay*

"With incisive honesty wrapped in deep compassion, Ericka Andersen brings to light a conversation many Christians have been having in silence for years. *Freely Sober* doesn't bring shame or deliver ultimatums; it offers a lamp on the path toward freedom. With surgical precision, Ericka blends scientific rigor and scriptural clarity to expose the deeper reasons why we drink and how we heal. Whether you're rethinking your own choices around alcohol or trying to understand those of someone you love, this book will feel like a long-overdue dose of hope."

W. Lee Warren, neurosurgeon and host of *The Dr. Lee Warren Podcast*

FREELY
SOBER

RETHINKING ALCOHOL
THROUGH THE LENS OF
——————— FAITH ———————

ERICKA ANDERSEN

ivp

An imprint of InterVarsity Press
Downers Grove, Illinois

InterVarsity Press
P.O. Box 1400 | Downers Grove, IL 60515-1426
ivpress.com | email@ivpress.com

InterVarsity Press® is the publishing division of InterVarsity Christian Fellowship/USA®. For more information, visit intervarsity.org.

Scripture quotations, unless otherwise noted, are from The Holy Bible, English Standard Version. ESV© Text Edition: 2016. Copyright © 2001 by Crossway Bibles, a publishing ministry of Good News Publishers. Used by permission. All rights reserved.

Published in association with the literary agency of Legacy, LLC, Winter Park, Florida, 32789.

While any stories in this book are true, some names and identifying information may have been changed to protect the privacy of individuals.

The publisher cannot verify the accuracy or functionality of website URLs used in this book beyond the date of publication.

Cover design: Faceout Studio, Tim Green
Interior design: Daniel van Loon
Cover image: © Tetra/Winslow Productions / Tetra Images via Getty Images
Interior images: © palau83 / iStock via Getty Images, © _human / iStock via Getty Images

ISBN 978-1-5140-1336-6 (print) | ISBN 978-1-5140-1337-3 (digital)

Printed in the United States of America ∞

Library of Congress Cataloging-in-Publication Data
Names: Andersen, Ericka author
Title: Freely sober : rethinking alcohol through the lens of faith / Ericka Andersen.
Description: Downers Grove, IL : IVP, 2025.
Identifiers: LCCN 2025026898 (print) | LCCN 2025026899 (ebook) | ISBN 9781514013366 paperback | ISBN 9781514013373 ebook
Subjects: LCSH: Alcoholics–Religious life | Alcoholism–Religious aspects–Christianity | Church work with alcoholics
Classification: LCC BV4596.A48 A53 2025 (print) | LCC BV4596.A48 (ebook) | DDC 261.8/32292–dc23/eng/20250829
LC record available at https://lccn.loc.gov/2025026898
LC ebook record available at https://lccn.loc.gov/2025026899

31   30   29   28   27   26 | 13   12   11   10   9   8   7   6   5   4   3   2   1

This book is dedicated to

JACOB AND ABBY.

CONTENTS

INTRODUCTION

FIFTEEN YEARS AGO, I sat in a moonlit room behind a locked door with a bottle of peach schnapps at my feet and a Bible on my desk, googling "How to quit drinking." It felt like watching an X-rated movie in secret or hoping a doorbell-ringing visitor wouldn't see I was home.

I could not be found out because then someone might *make* me stop drinking. And that couldn't be anyone's choice but mine.

My search surfaced a link for Alcoholics Anonymous (AA), and another for a British women's sobriety group. I clicked on the latter, but the website was clunky and hard to navigate. I tried searching for local AA meetings, but I was far too scared to actually attend one.

Alcoholism, or a "drinking issue," felt like a man's problem. That was the only way I'd known it—in family members, in friends of my parents, in movies, and on TV. AA was, after all, started by men and for men.

Women were the ones who were supposed to keep the men in check. They'd started the temperance movement. They barely had time to drink, since they were keeping the kids and the house and their jobs in order.

My examples of alcoholism were . . .

Johnny Cash in *Walk the Line.*

Michael Keaton in *Clean and Sober*.

Nicholas Cage in *Leaving Las Vegas*.

I devoured these movies, bitterly savoring a sense of connection to the characters' lack of control around alcohol. Did anyone else around me get it? I didn't know because I didn't ask.

In my own life, drinking too much at night and attempting to correct myself the following day with Gatorade, tall cups of cold water, Excedrin, and sweaty, toxin-coaxing long runs, was par for the course.

A couple of hours later, I'd feel fine. I'd tell myself it couldn't be that bad if I exercised, cared for my kids, and did my job. Later that night, I might colead Bible study or attend a worship night at church. It was a life of constant maintenance, plotting drinks, and pushing boundaries. I was on a tightrope teetering over a fire.

The women in the films weren't like me. They were always the strong, straight, and healthy ones—because they had to be.

They were June Cash, helping her husband get clean, or Lady Gaga as Ally in *A Star is Born*, watching Bradley Cooper self-destruct. They were like my grandmother when my grandpa was manning a police car by day and a whiskey bottle by night.

I couldn't find anyone like me, a Christian woman who was active in her faith but couldn't stop struggling with alcohol. It didn't help that no one talks about things like that. I wouldn't have known if one of my acquaintances did have a problem.

I wish I'd had this book back then. I no longer drink, but I'm not assuming you have the same ultimate goal. You probably won't quit drinking by the end of this book. I won't even tell you to try quitting.

For now, I just want you to read with an open mind and curious heart. I want you to invite God into this reading with you and ask him to move through the words. He knows the plans he has for you. This book is part of those plans.

Few books or accessible support communities existed when I started this journey, and for Christian women seeking faith-based resources, that's still the case (although it has improved in recent years). They say if a book you need doesn't exist, write it yourself. I had a feeling one day I'd be the one to do it, though I knew I'd have to figure it out for myself first.

After many fits and starts, failures and successes, I finally did that.

I'm so glad you picked up this book, whether it's for yourself or a loved one you want to support. You might be trying to determine if your drinking is a problem or if your habits reflect Christ well. With all the conflicting opinions on alcohol, you might be trying to get clear on what's okay and what's not and determine if you or a loved one should be concerned. You're asking questions like:

"Am I overthinking this, or is it really an issue worth wrestling with?"

"Alcohol doesn't disrupt my life, so is it a problem?"

You might go weeks without drinking much, but when you do— something doesn't feel right. You say things you wouldn't usually say, argue with your spouse, snap at your children, and treat your body disrespectfully by eating junk or avoiding exercise. Maybe you picture problem drinkers dumping vodka in their coffee mugs, driving under the influence, or constantly recovering from hangovers. That's not you, so why do you keep feeling drawn to evaluate your relationship with alcohol?

These questions keep resurfacing, tugging at your heart. Maybe it's time to look deeper. It could be a Holy Spirit conviction. And that won't go away until you handle it.

Maybe you're in a different place, like where I was: craving freedom from alcohol's grip on my mind and body, exhausted by the cycle of making promises to cut back or quit . . . only to break them days later.

Perhaps you've said things you regret, lost hours of restful sleep, and maxed out your anxiety. You've spent too many hours plotting, planning, moderating, and finally regretting the choice to drink—even when there weren't major consequences. You may feel like a hypocrite, but imagining a whole lifetime without alcohol sounds really hard. It's been a part of your life for many years by now.

In this book, we will walk through all of that—the conflicting thoughts and feelings—together. Struggling with alcohol as a woman of faith has its nuances. We also have our great God to lean on as we process and progress. Here, we'll talk about why we *really* drink, how it started, what it means, where God is in the midst of the struggle, and how simple perspective shifts can powerfully change the paradigm.

Back when I was googling resources in the dark of my room, there was so much I didn't know, bastions of wisdom I hadn't discovered yet. If I had known then what I do now, I wouldn't have felt so hopeless about the possibility of real change.

Over the last five years of sobriety, I've gathered hard-won insights, perspective shifts, and real-life lessons—things I now feel called to share with you. You don't know what you don't know. I earned many of the lessons and stories I share here in the aftermath of falling off the wagon and getting back up. What finally led me to lasting healing was learning to keep moving forward—even when I failed.

While I've not had a drink in more than five years, that's not the only success I want to share. It's merely the foundation of *many* other profound revelations, including an improved relationship with God, professional success, positive movement in my marriage, the ability to be a better mother, and being able to help thousands of people who've read my writing on sobriety in places like *The New York Times*, *The Wall Street Journal*, *Christianity Today*, and more.

My mission is to show you that there is a life without alcohol constantly sneaking into your thoughts, shaping your choices, and causing you grief and shame. There is a life where you don't question when, how much, or if you should drink at all. There is freedom from alcohol, no matter how little or much it currently affects you. That day will come.

By the end of this book, my hope and belief is that you will never think about alcohol in the same way again, that you won't walk away the same—because once you know, you can't unknow.

What you read here will empower you. New knowledge, fresh insights, and personal revelation can be transformational. And when you change your mindset about drinking, other parts of life begin to change for the better. Whatever you choose to do with your relationship with alcohol from here, you'll be equipped with the clarity and information to do it wisely.

Six years ago, I couldn't have imagined that I'd be at five years of sobriety and sharing all the details of that experience with others. At the time, I didn't know I was *this close* to the end of alcohol's hold on me.

I've walked with hundreds of people in my support group, and they can all relate to where you may be today. Some of them are ten years sober, some six months. Some are still drinking and working on it. There is no wrong place to connect with God and step forward in renewed hope:

Where shall I go from your Spirit?
Or where shall I flee from your presence?
If I ascend to heaven, you are there!
If I make my bed in Sheol, you are there!
If I take the wings of the morning
and dwell in the uttermost parts of the sea,
even there your hand shall lead me,
and your right hand shall hold me. (Psalm 139:7-10)

If you think you're hidden from God, you're under an illusion. We cannot flee from God's presence. In the biblical story of Hagar, the concubine who fled from her master's house after becoming pregnant with his child, God reveals that he remains with us even in our despair.

Hagar was so desperate that she ran away without a destination in mind. In her lowest moment, she called out to the Lord—and to her surprise, he answered her. In the dust of the desert where she was preparing to die, she gathered up what little faith she had left and threw it out there.

When God showed up, Hagar sparked to life again and said: "You are a God of seeing. . . . Truly, here I have seen him who looks after me" (Genesis 16:13).

He sees us and meets us wherever we are. He sees you and is ready to walk with you to the next step. I know this because I've lived it, and because there's evidence throughout human history of God walking with his people on the mountains and in the valleys. That doesn't change, because he is "the same yesterday, today and forever" (Hebrews 13:8). I see it more clearly than ever now. With the hard-won tools, insights, and wisdom I've gathered over the past five years, I know this path is possible for any woman willing to do what Hagar did—cry out to the Lord and trust that he sees her.

You've got an opportunity in your hands with this book. Read to the end and celebrate the small wins. I encourage you to read thoughtfully, complete the questions and exercises, and consider which resources might be good tools for you. Don't just read and walk away. Read with intention, believing that this can be the beginning of positive change in your relationship with alcohol, God, yourself, and others. Let this be the moment the tables turn.

ONE

LET'S COME CLEAN

EVER FEEL LIKE SOMETHING IS OFF with your alcohol consumption? It's *fine* (most of the time), but you have a nagging sense of discomfort. You flip open Scripture and see that drinking alcohol is within our liberties as Christians, but still—what is it about drinking that makes you feel bad sometimes? What is that inexplicable yet gnawing sense that refuses to disappear?

I know that feeling all too well. I lived it for at least fifteen years, and ignored it most of that time. If it feels familiar, you're in the right place. Step number one is beginning to think more deeply about what *could* be a problem, or what might be better for your life as a Christian woman when it comes to alcohol.

That quiet nudge—the one urging us to examine why alcohol doesn't sit right anymore—isn't something we should ignore. It's not random. Often, it's a nudge from God inviting us to take a closer look. Or it's a nudge from the body, pointing us in a wiser direction. The body holds more wisdom than we give it credit for; soon, we'll investigate exactly how alcohol affects the brain, the gut, the immune system, and more.

"For everything there is a season, and a time for every matter under heaven," says Ecclesiastes 3:1. Maybe now is the time to think about alcohol consumption deeply. It took me fifteen years to find the right time, but when that anointed interval came, things finally began to change.

I'm not asking you to quit drinking. That's not what this is about. It's also not about chasing the perfect amount of alcohol—some magical number of drinks per week that keeps you safely on the right side of an invisible line. I'm asking for your commitment to listen with an open heart and mind to what God wants to reveal to you in the next two hundred pages or so. So, we can remove the pressure to make drastic changes with alcohol right now. Instead, let's settle into the comfort of curiosity, knowledge, and exploration. In the meantime, I've got a story, some of which may be relatable.

This is how it always started.

After a long day of work, I'd pick up my one-year-old and three-year-old, wrestle them into car seats, soothe their end-of-day irritations with snacks and sippy cups, and return home to a sink full of dishes, a filthy carpet, and my cat's vomit on the kitchen floor.

My husband would be working late, meaning dinner was still mine to figure out. Who knew feeding children three meals a day could be such a monumental task? It wasn't something I'd considered before family life. It was a lot for a woman who doesn't enjoy cooking or meal planning.

Once we'd unload from the car, the baby would take a short nap. She often struggled to sleep, while my toddler loudly blared *Cocomelon* downstairs. As often as not, I'd have gotten into an argument with my husband over a text message (never a good way to converse!) and my job as a self-employed writer would feel overwhelming. In this season, I was postpartum, tired, and trying to do too much: write a book, host a podcast, and work full-time, all while dealing with undiagnosed ADHD. Looking back, I see how my self-deprivation led to a search for a fix. It's no wonder I sought relief from the chaos of a good, but overstimulated, life.

Most nights followed the same pattern. I'd reach instinctively for the wine after work. It was the norm. Too normal. Too frequent. Too much. I knew it—but couldn't seem to stop. As a devout, church-going Christian, it felt at times as if I was living a double life. The weight of it all had been building for years, but I couldn't think of one safe person to talk to about it.

I entirely blamed myself for giving in, thinking my habit was due to a weak character and limited faith. When it comes to the why and how of an unhealthy attachment to alcohol, there was so much I didn't know. I didn't know then that, according to the National Institute on Alcohol Abuse and Alcoholism (NIAAA), more than twelve million American women struggle with alcohol in some way. That data said I wasn't alone. But in these days, I didn't feel that way.

I also had no idea how drinking alcohol had chemically affected my brain. These daily drinking habits were basic training for future addiction—or unhealthy dependence at a minimum.

Consistent consumption, I later learned, had fooled my brain and body into thinking alcohol was *necessary* to survive the day. That may sound silly because, of course, we don't need alcohol to survive, but that sensation is entirely real within the body. *The Handbook of Clinical Neurology* describes what's called the "incentivize sensationalization theory," which speaks to this feeling of "need." The theory suggests that "chronic drug (e.g., alcohol)-related neuroadaptation sensitizes the reward circuit . . . significantly promot[ing] greater wanting, or the craving response, and increases risk of chronic alcoholism."

In other words, these habits are practice drills for addiction and dependence. Cravings, which make us feel that compulsive pull to drink, are self-created feelings driven by repeated exposure to an addictive substance like alcohol. This feeling only intensifies thanks to "increased sensitivity" to the brain's reward systems. We were built this way—it's a scientific fact.

In his book *Addiction and Virtue*, Kent Dunnington writes that we can capitulate to cravings when "hurry, strong appetite or an abnormal bodily state wrecks the deliberative process that is needed to arrive at a right judgment." He calls these addictive desires, or cravings, "indefatigably persistent," something that "pits a force of seemingly inexhaustible resources against a limited power, the human will."

Yeah, that hits.

There's a common acronym that helps people assess why they may act or feel a certain way: H.A.L.T. In a vulnerable moment, it's helpful to ask if I'm *hungry, angry, lonely,* or *tired.* Recognizing these categories can help clarify decision-making around alcohol, even if it doesn't make the destructive desire disappear.

I felt intense cravings every day, like clockwork—relentless and compulsive urges that felt nearly impossible to resist. My thoughts were loud, intrusive, and obsessive, almost like a sinister being whispering internal lies. They often drowned out God's quiet comfort, which might have drawn me out of the invisible prison I'd made. But I couldn't get these internal thoughts to cease. I needed some method or strategy to shush the oppressive chatter.

One thing about God: He never forces us to listen. As the Good Shepherd, he loves us enough to let us choose whether to accept his help. He doesn't shout or beg for our attention—he simply waits, gently and patiently. God once told the prophet Elijah to stand on the mountain and wait for him to speak. Elijah did as he was told, standing on the mountain and waiting for. . .what? He wasn't sure. He witnessed a wind and a fire and an earthquake, but Scripture says God was *not* in that wind or fire or earthquake.

After this environmental chaos ended, Elijah likely felt as if the world had turned upside down around him. And then he heard "the sound of a low whisper"—and *this* was the voice of God (1 Kings 19:12).

Like Elijah's moment on the mountainside, my life had gotten loud. The noise came from babies, work, marriage, anxiety, family turmoil, and so much more. It was so loud that I don't think I could hear what God was saying to me. This was the life I had always dreamed of, so why did it feel so hard? Why did I *want* to run to alcohol? Guilt for feeling this way consumed me and made everything even darker.

In a world that demands us to be and do so much, Christian women may particularly feel this pressure. After all, we're more harshly judged for our behavior and moral character. When we mess up, we're more likely to be called hypocrites, or even accused of causing doubt in others. Higher expectations seem to naturally exist for us, and with them comes an extra layer of shame when we fall short.

We carry a multitude of positions in life: mentor, mother, volunteer, wife, daughter, role model, or Bible study leader. Not only must we maintain societal appearances, but those same duties often get tagged as spiritual positions within the church. Everyone's watching—or so it feels that way. Although the church is meant to be a place where we can bring our burdens—and often is—it's easy to understand how the one little problem of drinking is something we'd rather keep to ourselves.

Recovery and sobriety groups like AA emphasize anonymity, which can be beneficial. However, there's a darker side to the promotion of anonymity. It can reinforce a sense of embarrassment about our struggle. It can reinforce the idea that revealing ourselves will just bring shame.

Unfortunately, shame has a way of compounding. One night, once dinner was done, diapers changed, and the day was behind us, things at home took a turn. I suddenly remembered a pair of mini wine bottles hidden behind the bathroom towels in the master bedroom. I literally salivated at the thought of them. Soon, I was frantically rummaging through the closet, pushing aside an old shower caddy, a nail kit, and scattered toiletries, praying the bottles were really still there.

They were there, stashed discreetly behind layers of terrycloth. I locked the bathroom door, turned on the faucet, unscrewed the cap, and gulped the bitter, lukewarm liquid without regard for taste. The warm, unsavory tanginess soon melted into a buzzy warmth in my chest. Watching myself in the mirror felt like viewing a documentary of someone else's life. Was this red-faced woman pathetically chugging hidden alcohol behind locked doors really me?

Just then, my daughter's cries rang out from her room, breaking the trance of my personal reality show. I walked in, scooped her out of the crib, and began to rock her again, temporarily relieved of my discomfort. I reveled in her little body snuggled against mine and sang her "Jesus Loves Me" until her eyes closed. Even after she was asleep, I stayed put in what felt like a perfect moment, there in the dark, holding onto the sweet feelings of the buzz from both alcohol and being heart-to-heart with my baby. The feeling was fleeting.

With wine in my system, everything felt lighter, faster, more manageable. The room was dark, but the buzz illuminated my mood. That first rush of intoxication is like flipping on Christmas lights inside your body. Everything felt dull and cold before, but with alcohol, the atmosphere shifted from gray to color, optimism, and relief. I achieved the feeling I sought, but it wouldn't last long—it never did.

My thoughts soon accelerated: Why did bedtime with little ones feel so hard? After tucking my daughter in, I was rattled out of my euphoric state by a shot of momentary panic. My mind raced:

What was I doing?

Who *does* this?

What kind of mother am I?

I had a beautiful baby girl to rock to sleep, and I needed alcohol to get through it?

I sang "Jesus Loves Me" while working up a buzz. It was gross, pathetic, embarrassing, disgusting. That's what I told myself, at least.

Looking back, I get emotional that I fogged up those priceless moments with a buzz, creating a barrier between myself and one of the most precious memories a mother can have with her child. The demons of shame circled my mind with raised pitchforks. Here's a literal thought that cropped up in my mind over and over again: "You're a big, fat piece of garbage." (Satan always throws "fat" in there for good measure.) The arrows pierced my head and heart. I knew it wasn't true, but I felt God had turned his face on me at that moment because of my bad decisions. I didn't put that on him; it was all on me. What a disappointment I was—again.

I'd forgotten the gospel of grace, which says that as believers, we "have now been justified by [Christ's] blood" (Romans 5:9). We are justified and covered, but our earthly minds can convince us otherwise in these moments. The truth is that our mistakes don't disqualify us. Jesus' blood perpetually cleanses, offering us a fresh start day in and day out. This undeserved grace, though often hard to grasp, is the bedrock of Christian hope, empowering us to choose a better path. It's part of the privilege of being a Christian. Thank God for that.

In my confusion, all I knew was that I wanted—*needed*—to escape this mental and spiritual assault. Obviously, more alcohol wouldn't solve the problem. Nevertheless, my feet moved forward as if guided by an unseen force. After laying my daughter back down, I returned to the bathroom and took another, shorter, chug from the second bottle. Then, I restored it to its hiding place behind the soap and shampoo, tiny soldiers guarding my precious resource. Sufficiently tipsy, I changed into pajamas and grabbed my phone for some blissful scrolling, hoping my husband wouldn't notice I never came downstairs to hang out.

Before dozing off, I chugged an obligatory glass of water and took two Excedrin, hoping to ward off a morning headache. I reasoned that *real* drunks would never remember to wash their face, brush their teeth, or drink water before passing out. These small routines helped me continue avoiding the reality of my problem.

Hours later, I lay in bed, consumed with guilt and anxiety, sleep slipping further away in the chaos of my mind. I thought about how alcohol was like a secret, abusive lover I couldn't seem to leave. Like a man who promises to leave his wife for his mistress, alcohol's assurances *always* returned void. What kind of weak woman returns for the lies? Again, self-hatred enveloped me as I considered how I might, somehow, someday, quit drinking for good.

As the minutes on my green-lit clock ticked by, I spiraled further into a mental hole of depression and shame. I had to do *something* to make myself feel better in the moment. Eventually, I got out of bed, grabbed the last bit of wine from the bathroom cupboard, dumped out the bottle, wrapped it in plastic bags, and trashed it. I chugged another glass of water and vowed I would quit drinking tomorrow. Everything was possible tomorrow.

The next day, the headache appeared despite the two glasses of water. Regret, fatigue, and a weak commitment to quit drinking again were also present. Like every other time I'd made the promise, it only lasted a few days. But things were coming to a head and I was one day closer to finally coming clean with myself and what it might take to quit drinking.

WHAT I LEARNED THAT CHANGED THE GAME

Scratch beneath the surface of alcohol's cultural veneer, and the revelations come quickly. Any romantic and nostalgic notions we had about alcohol's role in our lives quickly crumbles. We'll talk more about the historical and cultural narratives surrounding alcohol in later chapters.

For so many, we've depended on and misused alcohol because it's masked by a misnomer of fun and celebration. Singular moments and memories, often ones that are profound or magical, tend to be paired with drinking. A wedding, concert, vacation, holiday, or party—most every fun thing we do can and often does involve alcohol. That means we can cling to fond memories and easily ignore alcohol's harmful effects.

At the time of my deepest struggle, the supposed benefits of alcohol often came to my mind. Things like buzzy comfort after a long day, a socially acceptable escape from hardship, help in falling asleep, and at times, what felt like the only moment of relief in a trying day. It was hard to imagine letting go of the solution to so many temporary issues.

I wasn't comfortable calling myself a "problem drinker" or "alcoholic." Labels repelled me and kept me from working toward better choices. Many women feel the same way, unable to reconcile such a stereotyped categorization. But what about gray-area drinkers, those getting by but still questioning their dysfunctional relationship with alcohol? Where could they go without feeling stigmatized?

Those other descriptions seemed terrifying, final, ugly, and life-ruining. Nothing really bad had happened as a result of my drinking—yet. However, I knew that it could, that I played with fire every time I drank too much. I'm inviting you to consider your alcohol use without labels. You may be just a bit uncomfortable with your drinking; don't let labels stop you from exploring what could be different or better for you.

Don't just think about moments when you're drinking, perhaps attending a fun event. Rather, consider the entirety of the alcohol ecosystem and how it reverberates in wider ways for your body, spirit, and psyche. Recognizing the negative parts of alcohol won't erase the perceived positives—both can coexist. All I ask is for honesty about your full experience.

It took me some time to be truthful with myself. Even though I wasn't an "alcoholic," I told myself, something wasn't right.

If I could just not *want* to drink, everything would be fine. But there was no way to snap my fingers and make that happen.

I felt I couldn't share what I was thinking with anyone because that would mean I'd *have* to quit—or face being judged forever if anyone saw me drink again. This thought kept me from opening up for years. I also worried that if I *did* quit drinking, people would make untrue assumptions about me (and why I *had* to quit) as a woman, mother, and Christian. There seemed to be no good answer.

Growing up, I believed alcoholics and drug addicts lacked morality and self-control. They chose to indulge, and that was their fault. Those with "real" addiction issues were homeless, jobless, and faithless. They lost custody of their kids, drove into telephone poles, and drank liquor with breakfast. They walked around in a stupor each day before passing out on the couch.

I was so naive.

These created caricatures of those who struggle with alcohol or drugs are damaging and alienating. They also indicate that a struggle with substances is a moral failing that reflects the strength of one's faith, character, and potential.

When we see our battle with alcohol as a moral failing or write it off exclusively as sin, we discount the many nuances and realities of dependence and addiction. (I will discuss the question of alcoholism and sin in a later chapter.)

You will only find peace with this part of your life if you accept the reality of what it is for you—the good and bad parts. How has ignoring it worked out so far? How has hoping it would just quietly disappear been going? No matter how small or large an issue this is for you, it won't go away if you don't face it head on. If you need to hide this book with a fake cover or read it on Kindle to keep the topic private, do it. What matters is facing this struggle—for your future, your testimony, God's glory, and the next generation which we pray won't have to fight the same battle.

The path to freedom from alcohol isn't a straight line. It was liberating when I realized this wasn't a battle of wills, in which I could try hard enough and overcome once and for all. I wasn't storing up the nerve to say "no" forever on one particular day. Finally, I realized the real battle wasn't between me and the glass, choosing to pick it up or walk on by. The real battle was in my heart.

You can't fight a spiritual battle with willpower or discipline. It's a holy war requiring supernatural tools found in the Holy Spirit. The Holy Spirit not only provides the "tools" we need but is also actively at work within us to will and to act.

We know this from Philippians 2:13 (NLT), which reads, "For God is working in you, giving you the desire and the power to do what pleases him."

Victory doesn't come from the tools alone, but from the Holy Spirit empowering us from within—giving us both the desire and the power to do what pleases God.

As Christians, anything that *might* be an idol will require surrender.

Consider where you are now. The question remains: Do you want to stay here? Is alcohol worth fighting for? Can you imagine something better? Would your life be better or worse with less alcohol? With none? These are thoughts I reluctantly grappled with in the beginning. I didn't force myself to quit drinking; I just let myself learn. I needed permission to explore and reach authentic conclusions honestly. I'm inviting you to do the same.

WHAT I DIDN'T KNOW THEN

In my assessments of alcohol's impact, the night with my daughter was one of my lowest. The evening felt familiar—I'd been here before. But this time, a stark awareness cut through the routine, revealing how deeply this problem had taken hold.

In hindsight, I can see God working supernaturally through unspecial, nondescript moments. Paul assures us that even as we feel powerless to change, he can use our weakest areas to begin shaping everything for "the good of those who love him" (Romans 8:28 NIV).

As it was, I struggled in isolation. Therefore, I was ignorant of many tools and resources to help me make changes and relieve my fear.

What I didn't know *was* hurting me:

- I didn't know that you could quit drinking without calling yourself an alcoholic.

- I didn't know that you could share that you *want* to quit drinking even if you haven't quit yet.

- I didn't realize that God wasn't angry with me for drinking, and that I had the freedom to quit without carrying the weight of conditional love.

- I didn't know that, according to the National Institutes of Health (NIH), over five million American women have alcohol use disorder, and most of them hide it.

I had heard that in AA meetings, you had to say, "Hi I'm Ericka and I'm an alcoholic." Turns out, you actually *don't* have to do that. And there are many more programs out there today besides AA.

The standard narrative didn't turn out to be true. Who knew?

GETTING CURIOUS CHANGED EVERYTHING

It's remarkable how long I stayed rooted in a problem based on false assumptions and wrong information.

Being "sober curious" was the catalyst for shifting my perspective in a life-changing direction. Being sober curious means asking questions about drinking—yours, theirs, and everyone's. It means educating yourself about alcohol and asking insightful questions about how drinking affects you and those around you—without judgment.

I was sober curious for years before hearing the phrase. A few public-facing individuals were brave enough to share their stories online, but that was uncommon.

If someone mentioned they'd quit drinking in a blog post or social media share, I would binge their feeds for more insight. Hearing the stories of others who were like me was essential for believing that I, too, could do this. One day, after reading a blogger's post about her ten years of sobriety, I emailed her. It was the first time I'd ever admitted to anyone that I *might* have a problem.

My heart raced as I typed, each word heavier than the last. When I finally hit send, a wave of uncertainty washed over me, as if I had just exposed a fundamental secret. But I knew it was a necessary first step toward understanding what might be possible for me. As I expressed my fears, my words were cautious, tentative, and almost apologetic. Her response was kind and encouraging—she reassured me that it was worth exploring if I thought I had a problem. That slight, compassionate nudge felt like a lifeline. It would be years before I'd quit drinking, but looking back, that minor step was ultimately critical.

I had a long way to go. As a Christian, I'd attempted so many things already:

- Aimed to pray the desire away by writing prayers and copying Scriptures like "I can do all things through him who strengthens me" (Philippians 4:13).
- Played a recording of the worship song "Oceans" so often I thought it would *actually* make my faith strong enough to overcome
- Read Brene Brown's *The Gifts of Imperfection*
- Watched multiple TED Talks about sobriety
- Posted notecard affirmations on my computer screens and bathroom mirror
- Gritted my way through a social event or two without drinking (but it was torture!)
- Done a thirty-day cleanse
- Attempted to live by rules of moderation: "only drink on the weekend" or "no more than two drinks at special events (I mean, definitely no more than three)"

Still, the "wine witch" (the name many sober people use for the voice that compels them to drink) remains rooted in our minds, always returning to whisper a justification for "just one drink" in our ear.

You deserve it.
Everyone does it.
Just for tonight.
You only live once.
Life is hard.
You're not hurting anyone.

At times, it felt like I was watching myself make wrong choices. I'd see myself get off the couch, walk to the fridge, pour the glass, and sit back down. I knew I shouldn't do it, but I knew that I would—and felt utterly powerless to stop it.

Romans 7:15 seemed applicable most days: "I do not understand my own actions. For I do not do what I want, but I do the very thing I hate."

Paul, you have no idea . . .

Maybe you're like I was, and the strategies and tactics haven't solved your problem. You're still thinking about it, wishing it away, desperate to be a normal drinker who can have fun, stop at one, and not wake up hating yourself or just regretting that you gave in—again.

Killing the voice in our minds that urges us to drink is more complicated than just saying no. It's part sinful human nature, part neuroscience, part sanctification, and part determination. That's quite the pie chart. And it really isn't about the wine.

Why would a rational person choose to do something they know is ultimately harmful? And how harmful does something need be to be worth quitting? The old debate—whether addiction is a disease or a choice—misses the mark. It's far more complex than having no power or complete control. In approaching the subject of our addictions with nuance and curiosity, we can create new frameworks and ideas about how to think about them, which will lead us to better choices and outcomes.

But just as quick changes rarely free us from our addictions, neither can information or habit changes *on their own* break the powerful hold of alcohol. Addiction and dependence are heart issues, deeply rooted in our psyches and intertwined with our very beings after years of facing the world with a bottle in hand. Without the inner work, the outer work is another mask, destined to fail when we fall prey to emotional and spiritual downfalls.

That inner work is how we discover why we do what we do, which is what leads to meaningful change. Wouldn't it be great to know why you get these powerful, unwanted feelings?

Learning that we turn to drink because of a desire to achieve joy, fulfillment, and community can help us process things in a healthier way. Those desires aren't bad, in and of themselves. So, how can we seek them out in better ways?

When we understand why we drink within the context of our full, complex lives, we can transform our habits, overcome cravings, and gain a broader perspective on God's purpose for our lives.

Our good desires are valid and can be fulfilled more deeply through holistic solutions that cultivate true human flourishing. Instead of alcohol, we can invest in authentic relationships, raw honesty with God, setting boundaries, leaving toxic situations, healing childhood wounds, and wrestling with uncomfortable truths.

PAUSE & ASSESS

Take a few minutes to ask yourself the following questions and record your answers. Write what comes to mind, and don't judge yourself for your answers.

Physical and Practical Impact: How does my drinking impact my health and other resources?

☐ Do I often feel physically drained, mentally foggy, or unable to be fully present because of drinking? If so, how does that affect me in practical ways?

☐ Is alcohol negatively affecting my health in any ways I'm aware of? For example, sleep disruption, sex drive or response, blood sugar, metabolism, dehydration, energy, or headaches?

☐ How much of my time, money, or resources go toward drinking, and is that aligned with the stewardship God calls me to?

Faith Life: Does alcohol bring me closer to God, or does it create distance in my relationship with him?

☐ Does my drinking help me display the fruits of the Spirit (love, joy, peace, patience, kindness, goodness, faithfulness, gentleness, self-control), or does it undermine them?

☐ How often do I ask for forgiveness related to my drinking—whether for losing control, damaging relationships, or neglecting responsibilities?

☐ Am I fully convinced that drinking aligns with God's best intention for me, or do I feel a sense of conviction I've been trying to ignore?

☐ If I prayed, "Lord, show me what you want for my life when it comes to alcohol," would I truly be willing to follow his answer?

☐ How do I feel about the idea of being completely free from alcohol? Does that thought fill me with relief, fear, or resistance—and why?

Relationships: How does my drinking affect my role as a sister, friend, daughter, wife, or mother? Does it enhance or hurt my ability to serve and love others well?

☐ What example am I setting for my children, family, or church community about how Christians handle stress, celebrate, or cope with pain?

☐ Does alcohol ever cause tension, conflict, or disappointment in my relationships with those I love?

☐ Have I ever worried that I might make a serious mistake due to being intoxicated that could harm—physically or emotionally—someone I love? How often?

Emotional and Mental Well-Being: When I reflect on my emotional health, does alcohol seem to amplify my burdens or lighten them?

☐ How does drinking affect my mood in the moment, for better or for worse?

☐ Do I feel freer, calmer, or more at peace after drinking, or do I feel shame, anxiety, and regret?

☐ Do I ever use alcohol to cover more profound struggles like stress, loneliness, resentment, or exhaustion?

☐ If you have any diagnosed mental health struggles: Does drinking ultimately improve my mental health struggles or make them worse?

Professional Life and Calling: Does my drinking help me achieve my purpose in life or hinder me?

☐ If you work outside the home: Has my drinking ever negatively impacted my performance at work? If so, how? How often?

☐ When I think about my goals for my life and the legacy I want to leave, how does my drinking fit in? Does it help me achieve those things or distract or even hinder me?

☐ If I consider my future self, the woman I hope to be in Christ, does she still drink?

TWO

SHOULD CHRISTIANS EVEN DRINK?

SHOULD CHRISTIANS DRINK alcohol at all? Is it sinful to do so? Scripture unequivocally condemns drunkenness and acknowledges how destructive it can be. That's probably why Christians have debated if they *should* drink alcohol for over two hundred years. Unfortunately, the answer isn't simple.

For most of history, it wasn't really up for debate. Throughout the first eighteen hundred years of the church, Christians regularly consumed alcohol as a part of daily life. There were no fancy cocktails or margaritas back then, but beer and wine were common forms of community and celebration.

Wine in particular was associated with many good, godly things, often presented to God at the altar and meant as an emblem of spiritual blessing and cheer. "All the best of the oil and all the best of the wine and of the grain, the firstfruits of what they give to the LORD, I give to you," reads Numbers 18:12. Abraham blesses his son with "an abundance of grain and new wine" (Genesis 27:28 NIV). In the Psalms, we read of wine that will "gladden the heart of man" (Psalm 104:15). Wine plays a starring role in Jesus' first miracle at the wedding in Cana (John 2). This wasn't an accident.

29

In this case, water-turned-wine represents new life in Christ and, ultimately, his blood atonement for us on the cross.

These things are true, but it's also important to note that wine today and wine in Jesus day were not always the same. In the blog post "Was New Testament Wine Alcoholic?" the Center for Faith and Culture tells us that, in ancient times, wine was often diluted with water or unfermented. People often drank wine as a substitute for water, which was difficult to purify. Additionally, due to ancient fermentation and storage methods, the alcohol content was significantly lower than it is today. In other words, this isn't your mama's wine cooler. Undiluted wine was available for special occasions, but much of the time, people drank this lower-alcohol beverage, which had little risk of leading to drunkenness. Given all the negative verses about drunkenness, Jesus would not have been encouraging his people to become drunk.

Christian history is also spotted with positive associations with alcohol. In 1779, Arthur Guinness opened his first pub in Dublin; he used the income to fund Christian charities and hospitals. Around the same time, Spanish Catholics planted vineyards at their missions on the coast of California. When we associate wine with this kind of warmth, celebration, and faith, it can be difficult to grasp why it has harmed us and those we love.

Rumbling against alcohol began in the early 1800s, when we see the first recorded sermon warning against the sins of alcohol consumption: "The Fatal Effects of Ardent Spirits" by the Reverend Ebenezer Porter. In the printed copies of his sermon, Porter revealed what led him to write it: "In the winter of 1805, a transient man perished in the snow, with a bottle of spirits at his side, about a mile from the meeting house, in this place. In consequence . . .

the following discourse was delivered to my own people." Like so many, his personal experience with the damning effects of alcohol moved him to speak on it.

"It may be safely affirmed that in this country, if in no other, it has proved a greater foe to human life and happiness than war, pestilence and famine," wrote Porter. Soon after that sermon, anti-alcohol movements began, including the Women's Christian Temperance Movement in 1874. From there, debates about alcohol consumption in the church began to rage. They continue to this day.

So, are Christians at liberty to drink alcohol without sinning?

Paul doesn't deny that "all things are lawful for me," but he urges Christians to seek what is truly beneficial (1 Corinthians 6:12). Within the complex freedom of the gospel, we're still responsible for our choices.

Humans are uniquely convicted and conscience driven. On the *Desiring God* podcast, John Piper summed it up this way:

> The first answer that I would give to the question "Is it a sin to drink alcohol?" is the same answer I give to the question "Is it a sin to drink water?" And the answer is that it could be.
>
> Drinking water when you should be giving a glass to someone else in need—that is sin. Drinking water when you should be paying more reverence to the preaching of God's Word—that is a sin. Drinking water when someone just warned you that it is contaminated and might kill you— that is sin. So drinking water can be sin.

Piper's comparison illustrates that alcohol consumption may be sinful for an individual based on their circumstances. What's the *why* behind your drink? As Scripture says, some things may be permissible, but "not all things are helpful." More importantly, Paul writes that we should "not be dominated by anything."

The line between drinking and drunkenness is crucial. However, like the unmarried couple who asks "How far is too far?" in their physical relationship, it matters deeply why we're asking about this line. Are we asking to toe the line of sin? The Bible says to "resist" sin—not to get close enough to touch it without doing so (James 4:7).

The difference between enjoying wine with dinner and a compulsion to drink—to *use* alcohol rather than just have it—matters here.

Like most things, alcohol may be permissible, but it's not always good. Consider:

Sex outside of marriage is a sin—not sex.

Gluttony is a sin—not eating.

Lusting is a sin—not attraction.

Drunkenness is a sin—not drinking.

What is meant for good, when taken in excess, can be bad. As Piper argued, even drinking water can be sinful depending on the circumstance. Alcohol is not forbidden, but it is to be taken very seriously considering what's at stake when we drink. In a sermon, Charles Spurgeon called drunkenness "the devil's back door to hell" and said if someone "gives away his brains to drink," he is "ready to be caught by Satan for anything."

The sin of drunkenness has never been up for debate. As often as the Bible mentions wine in holy and celebratory ways, it condemns drunkenness among the worst of sins. We read about intoxication leading to violence, destruction, and even eternal ruin. In Galatians 5:21, Paul warns against drunkenness, saying, "Those who do such things will not inherit the kingdom of God." Later, he says that "drunkards" will not "inherit the kingdom of God" (1 Corinthians 6:10). And he writes to Titus instructing "older women" not to be "slaves to much wine" (Titus 2:3).

Many people have seen such ruin in their own families or lives. Men with drinking problems are six times more likely to abuse their partners, according to Rongqin Yu and Alejo Nevado-Holgado in *PLOS Medicine*. Children of alcoholics are four times more likely to become alcoholics, according to the Los Angeles County Department of Mental Health. Rates of children in foster care rise yearly due to increased use of drug and alcohol abuse, according to authors Kristin Sepulveda and Sarah Catherine Williams for the Child Trends blog.

We can consider other scriptural evidence. Paul instructs Christians not to "put a stumbling block or hindrance in the way" of another (Romans 14:13). And as a mood and mind-altering drug, alcohol can detract from the full sober-mindedness Peter calls us to (1 Peter 5:8). Moreover, Scripture says that the body is a "temple of the Holy Spirit," which means we should treat our bodies as such (1 Corinthians 6:19). Bible teacher Phylicia Masonheimer writes in the blog post "Should Christians Drink Alcohol?" that every "entity that housed God's Spirit—the tabernacle, the Ark of the Covenant, and Solomon's temple—was meticulously crafted from the very best materials, consecrated in ceremonial splendor, and set apart for holy use." Today, God's Spirit inhabits our physical bodies (whoa!), and drunkenness dishonors that presence, corrupting the work he would do through us. Masonheimer rightly notes that "we tend to take our status as God's Spirit-bearers far too lightly." The sin of excessive drinking—even if it's accidental—can damage our witness. "Too much alcohol alters our mental and spiritual capabilities, limiting our ability to choose holiness—our most important responsibility as representatives of Christ on earth," says Masonheimer.

A HISTORICAL BATTLE

Many Bible passages directly address the pitfalls and curses of wine. Isaiah 5:11 warns, "Woe to those who rise early in the morning, that they may run after strong drink, who tarry late into the evening as wine inflames them!"

On the other hand, other verses relate wine to merriment and goodness. Ecclesiastes 9:7 instructs us, "Go, eat your bread with joy, and drink your wine with a merry heart, for God has already approved what you do." When we interpret Scripture, context, historical detail, and perspective are everything.

When I first started thinking seriously about dropping alcohol, I was also reading through the entire Bible for the first time. It's no coincidence that during this time period, I finally began to make progress spiritually and physically. Every time the Bible mentioned drunkenness (at least seventy times, depending on translation!), I was keenly aware of the (mostly) negative connotations.

The Levites, who were set apart as priests and community leaders, were instructed not to drink wine at all. "When you enter the Tent of Meeting, don't drink wine or strong drink, neither you nor your sons, lest you die," reads Leviticus 10:9 (MSG). Risking drunkenness or foolishness wasn't worth it while the Levites represented God.

Numerous episodes in Scripture (and in everyday life) illustrate that drinking alcohol is a slippery slope, even if you don't plan on being drunk. One of the most well-known Bible stories is that of Noah, who God called to build an ark before flooding the Earth. A lesser-known part of Noah's life comes after the flood, when the Bible says he disgraced himself in drunkenness:

> Noah began to be a man of the soil, and he planted a vineyard. He drank of the wine and became drunk and lay uncovered in his tent. And Ham, the father of Canaan, saw the nakedness of his father and told his two brothers outside. Then Shem and Japheth took a garment, laid it on both their shoulders, and walked backward and covered the nakedness of their father. (Genesis 9:20–23)

Instead of covering his father's shame, Ham went to gossip about it to his brothers. For this reason, in the aftermath of the incident, Noah cursed Ham, beginning many generations of significant brokenness and family division. It doesn't sound all that different from how drunkenness can affect families today.

It's easy to envision the scenario playing out. Maybe you can't imagine such an extreme event for yourself, but smaller instances of shame or regret may come to mind. The time you said too much, started an unnecessary argument, snapped at your kid, made a promise you couldn't keep. Drunkenness (including just being "buzzed") reveals unredeemed parts of us to the world. Those parts we'd rather hide away? Too much alcohol makes them transparent. Drunkenness is a backstabber, causing us to lie, betray, expose, and disgrace ourselves in one way or another.

In Proverbs 23, God warns against indulgence in wine:

Who has woe? Who has sorrow?
Who has contentions? Who has complaints?
Who has wounds without cause? Who has redness of eyes?
Those who linger long at the wine,
Those who go in search of mixed wine.
Do not look on the wine when it is red,
When it sparkles in the cup,
When it swirls around smoothly;
At the last it bites like a serpent,
And stings like a viper.
Your eyes will see strange things,
And your heart will utter perverse things.
Yes, you will be like one who lies down in the midst of the sea,
Or like one who lies at the top of the mast, saying:
"They have struck me, but I was not hurt;
They have beaten me, but I did not feel it.
When shall I awake, that I may seek another drink?"
(Proverbs 23:29-35 NKJV)

Honestly, I didn't know that was in Scripture until recently, but it's pretty spot on. Woe? Check. Sorrow? Check. Contentions? Check. Complaints? Check. Wounds without cause? Check. Redness of eyes? Check. Seeing strange things? Check. Uttering perverse things? Check. Not feeling physical pain? Check. Asking for another drink? Check, check.

Back then, reading through the Bible didn't lead me to quit drinking entirely. But it did empower me to educate myself and get honest about *why* I drank, and what it might take to overcome this destructive dependence. God has left no question marks when it comes to the sin of drunkenness. There are certain things the Bible never mentions at all, which doesn't mean God has no opinion on them. But Scripture is filled with commentary on this sin.

SHIFT YOUR EYES

Because excessive drinking is so normalized in our culture, some of Scripture's teachings can seem shocking to read. Consider Paul's teaching in 1 Corinthians, which names "drunkards" among the likes of adulterers, thieves, and idolators who will not "inherit the kingdom of God" (1 Corinthians 6:10). He goes on to write: "And such were some of you. But you were washed, you were sanctified, you were justified in the name of the Lord Jesus Christ and by the Spirit of our God" (1 Corinthians 6:11).

The Christian life should be transformative, and drunkenness is antithetical to the work of the Holy Spirit in our lives. That doesn't mean you're not a real Christian if you've been drunk. But it does mean that you've limited the transforming work of God in your life. Overindulgence in drink is like putting ourselves back into "old wineskins"—the person we were before Christ.

Why does alcohol have such a devastating effect on the spiritual life? As a mood-altering drug that affects the areas of the brain responsible for inhibition and decision-making, alcohol can make it easier to act against our own moral standards causing us to do or say something regrettable. Alcohol's effect also has a pronounced spiritual dimension. A buzz or intoxication, for a moment, may quench our heart's desire for some kind of feeling. By filling that desire with alcohol, we leave no room or space for the Holy Spirit to fill that need. It also opens the door for attacks from the enemy.

In an article on Christians and alcohol in a 1979 issue of *Christianity Today*, Barbara Thompson wrote:

> As followers of Jesus, we are involved in spiritual warfare and constantly facing temptations. Even when we are at our best, when our inhibitions are in full force, it is often difficult to resist the subtle stratagems of Satan. To deliberately lower our inhibitions, in a time of warfare, is quite foolish.

I'm thankful that as Christians we have individual liberties on many issues, including drinking. As Jesus told us, "If the Son sets you free, you will be free indeed" (John 8:36). But that means that the issue of alcohol is one to consider in conversation with God seriously. We *do* have immense freedom in Christ, but it's worth asking with a spirit of curiosity: Is drinking truly leading to a life of freedom? Or is it becoming a form of captivity?

While we're debating whether or not drinking alcohol is permissible, the divine work of God's plan is playing out around us. Let's be careful not to allow alcohol to distract us from the gospel mission or invite disunity.

We have the right to drink alcohol, but when we do—is it beneficial? Is it helpful? Does it glorify God? Does it seek the good of others? Contribute to our calling to be witnesses for Christ? Sometimes it does, but this is a serious, authentic conversation between you and God. Consider the abundant life Jesus promised. Is that a life of addiction or drunkenness? Is that a life in which we rely on alcohol as a stress reliever, social lubricant, or way to numb out?

PAUSE & REFLECT

- What new things did you learn about the history of alcohol in the Bible in this chapter? What was surprising or enlightening to remember (if you already knew)?
- Consider your own drinking habits. When are they beneficial? When are they not beneficial? Why?
- Do you view alcohol as being a part of spiritual warfare for you? If so, how? If not, why not?

THREE

THE PRESSURES WE FACE AS WOMEN

ONE THING I KNOW FOR SURE: It's easy to mask a dependence on alcohol as a busy, high-functioning woman who displays outward poise. We wake up early, hit the gym, get the kids to school, work full-time, make dinner, never miss church, volunteer on the weekends, take care of the dog. Surely, *that* woman couldn't have an issue with alcohol.

Our desire to unwind and seek comfort is natural. You often hear this about kids—they hold it together at school, only to unravel at home where they feel safe. Adults do this, too, but when alcohol enters the picture, it can be destructive. Yet, even as things spiral, we maintain a polished, public-facing persona. Long term, that outward maintenance merely compounds the problem.

WOMEN ARE AT HIGHER RISK

Given the realities of womanhood more generally, it's unsurprising to learn that women in high-stress jobs fare worse when it comes to alcohol abuse.

Up to 15 percent of practicing female physicians will develop substance abuse issues in their lifetimes, according to American

Addiction Centers (AAC), with the number rising to 25 percent for female surgeons. Similarly, a Bloomberg Law study found that over 50 percent of female lawyers have dealt with alcohol abuse. These numbers are far higher than the men in the same fields of work. This matches up with the increase in drinking among women more widely across the United States, according to the Centers for Disease Control and Prevention (CDC).

What's going on with the women? In their 2023 "Parenting in America Today" study, Pew Research found that mothers are more likely than fathers to say parenting is "stressful and tiring," feel more "judged," and worry more about hardships their children may face. The majority of mothers and fathers admit that moms carry the burden of managing their children's schedules, cleaning the house, helping with homework and feeding, bathing, and diaper changing.

We may live in a modern world, but women generally shoulder more simultaneous and consistent daily tasks for the family, often on top of having a full-time job. I don't say this to complain about womanhood or motherhood, but just to convey how women may feel added pressures. "Between being the primary breadwinner, the primary housekeeper, and trying to raise a four-year-old, I have no idea how I'm keeping it together," one woman noted in a private group. "I feel like I'm about to break . . . I go to work for ten hours, come home, clean, get our daughter to bed, and I'm left with maybe two hours, which I spend in pure anxiety and avoidance mode."

I'm not accusing dads of trying to complicate things. But we can be honest that old habits die hard. Some women enjoy some of those extra tasks. For example, keeping track of doctor's appointments and school events doesn't bother me. I like volunteering for classroom activities and keeping my kitchen clean each night. (Maybe I'm an outlier there.) Regardless, those invisible burdens can quietly tax us both mentally and emotionally. "It's so hard to break this habit when I don't know how to handle my problems," writes one woman in a Facebook group. "I go into a deep depression, but if I drink, it just seems so much easier to maintain my life."

As high-achieving women, model moms, and ministry leaders, we can put on an Instagram-ready façade that stands up to real life. And it's easy to excuse an issue with alcohol when no one seems to notice. Just because you're keeping things in check on the home front, with all the dominoes upright for now, doesn't mean this status quo glorifies God or leads to flourishing. Nor does alcohol contribute positively to one's mental or physical health. The health consequences of alcohol consumption are rarely discussed. But plenty of evidence notes the devastation, and the public is finally taking notice.

Only recently did the American Cancer Society change their recommendation for cancer prevention from having one glass of wine a day to entirely abstaining from alcohol. Here's how they put it in their "Alcohol Use and Cancer" explainer: "Drinking alcohol increases the risk of cancer. In fact, alcohol use is one of the most important preventable risk factors for cancer, along with tobacco use and excess body weight. Alcohol use accounts for about 5% of all cancers and 4% of all cancer deaths in the United States."

In the *International Journal of Epidemiology*, a team of researchers led by Seungyoun Jung and Molin Wang analyzed twenty studies looking at links between alcohol and breast cancer.

They found that drinking alcohol increased the risk of certain types of breast cancer by up to 35 percent. The CDC warns women that drinking alcohol can lead to a higher risk for liver disease, a decrease in brain function, heart muscle damages, fertility problems, and more risk for sexual violence ("Alcohol Use Effects on Men's and Women's Health").

Even without all the other factors that play into drinking, the physical and medical effects alone are enough reason to seriously reconsider.

WE'VE BEEN HOLDING THINGS
TOGETHER FOR A LONG TIME

Historically, women have held boundaries on drunkenness and disorderly conduct in men. Women started the temperance movement and did what was required to keep families together and children safe from the epidemic of alcoholism among men.

Women have often been seen as the moral bastions of society, representing and upholding virtue in their families and the community. These deep-seated ideas shape cultural expectations around acceptable behavior for women, such as drinking. Victorian novels and classic plays tend to cast pure women as a source of goodness and redemption to temper the vices of wayward men. In the same portrayals, "fallen" women are seen as shameful and irredeemable. In these acts, even a single transgression can hold the threat of lifelong ruin. But men aren't written the same. They've historically been allotted a measure of rebellion, often making bad choices, but ultimately allowed to remain the hero.

Even today, women's pain isn't always taken seriously, as women who've experienced years of painful diseases like endometriosis will tell you. They're told their pain is stress or anxiety or all in their head. They've been prescribed antidepressants when what they needed was surgery to remove painful cysts. They're told to deal with it instead of being given the proper tests to get to the root of a genuine issue. Historically, women have received lobotomies or been institutionalized when facing mental illness, anxiety, or even insomnia. (Oddly, men rarely received the same treatments.) The medical establishment has tended to advise women to numb their troubles via pill, surgery, or alcohol, rather than diagnosing the root cause.

Furthermore, the unique pressures of motherhood and womanhood require more women to perform in a male-dominated world, including the societal pressures to remain evermore thin, youthful, and pleasant.

Any emotional wounds or painful experiences we carry from the past intensify this. Everyone has memories of stress, fear, or hardship that stay with them. These experiences can have lasting effects on our well-being and shape the choices we make. But when we know the past and can dissect our trauma—from childhood, relationships, and culture—we can then have compassion for ourselves and begin to unlock the door to healing. We can recognize that womanhood and manhood come with unique pressures and challenges.

The world's most famous, lasting, and successful recovery program, Alcoholics Anonymous (AA), was created for and by men. Women didn't have the same opportunities as men to admit their addiction struggles openly, and treatment was out of the question. Sadly, that legacy of secrecy and lack of resources lives on today. Things are improving, but female-centric resources or recovery groups are still less common. The spirit of that historical stigma for women who struggle with addiction is alive.

However, many women have stepped forward for us. Margaret "Marty" Mann was a well-known socialite and advertising executive who was friends with Virginia Woolf. Mann's alcoholism resulted in homelessness, hospitalization, and suicide attempts. In 1939, she broke a barrier by attending an AA meeting; she became the first woman to achieve continuous sobriety from participation in the program. Her public admission of alcoholism and encouragement to others to seek help spurred the growth of AA for the first time among women.

Even Mann had predecessors paving the way. In an article for *Monument*, "A Brief History of Women in Alcohol Recovery," journalist Sarah duRivage-Jacobs wrote about the last two hundred years of women in recovery. She reported that as early as 1751, one of the first known support groups for women emerged within an Indigenous community, led by a Native American woman known as Wyoming Woman. These gatherings, called "recovery circles," were among the earliest forms of "recovery mutual-aid societies."

In the academic journal *Addictive Behaviors*, a team led by Audrey Hang Hai and Sehun Oh argue that these circles laid the foundation for modern recovery movements for both men and women, emphasizing the communal aspect of healing—a principle still central to groups like AA. While Wyoming Woman's recovery circles primarily served Native American women, they helped establish a framework that would later expand to support women nationwide. Meanwhile, alcohol use among White women in the newly formed United States nearly tripled between 1780 and 1820.

The gender disparity—how the female struggle with alcohol was viewed differently than males—is apparent when you consider stereotypical narratives from history and today. When a man drinks too much, his choices might be pegged as a legitimate way to struggle with the pressure of life and supporting a family. Conversely, a woman's overdrinking may be explained as a fundamental failure of character or morality. A study led by Abigail Riemer and Sarah Gervais, published in the journal *Sex Roles*, found women who drink are judged more harshly on their perceived humanity and intelligence. In another study, researcher Carly Lightowlers of the University of Liverpool found that "women are twice as likely as men to receive harsher sentences for assault offences when alcohol is a contributory factor."

We aren't living in the eighteenth century anymore, but a narrative persists that drinking is a man's issue which women just shouldn't have. This narrative produces hidden biases that order our thinking on issues of addiction. It leads to a deep sense of isolation for women struggling with alcohol; they may legitimately be judged more harshly than men. The stigma and fear of societal judgment can trap us in cycles of shame and secrecy. We're told, "Drink to relax—unless you have a problem." Then, hide it and don't tell anyone. That's the message we get from society.

CHRISTIAN WOMEN'S PARTICULAR VULNERABILITY

For Christian women, the message is even harder to decipher.

Christian women are expected to be and do so much. Frankly, pressures are high for Christians of both sexes. If we're not perfect, many of us fear we'll be seen as hypocrites or cause other Christians to struggle.

There's an extra layer of shame because it feels like everything we do is divinely tagged as faith leadership. Christian women bear incredible responsibility within the church itself. In their 2011 "State of the Church" report, Barna Research noted that "Women have traditionally been the backbone of volunteer activity in churches." That may be true, but Lifeway's "State of Ministry to Women" report found that few women who work in churches are ever paid. According to the report, of a sample of 842 women working in evangelical church ministries, only 17 percent received pay. Volunteering is important and essential in the life of a church, but like at home, women's efforts can easily go unseen or underappreciated even if they perform them with a joyful heart.

We also play a vital role in raising children (ours and others') of faith, keeping our families involved, and helping things run smoothly behind the scenes. For these reasons, Christian mothers can be judged even more harshly for struggling with addiction.

LEARNING FOR MYSELF

In due time, being controlled by alcohol was more exhausting than confronting the pain that drove me to it in the first place. Ultimately, one truth swung the pendulum for me: These internal struggles would be hard if I were drinking to avoid them; they would also be hard if I were working through them in healthier ways. The question was: Which kind of difficulty led to a flourishing life? Just asking the question reveals the answer.

The path of least resistance today can lead to greater challenges down the road. Whether you rely on a couple of glasses of wine on the weekends or finish a bottle each night, this is the moment to pause, reflect, and choose a different path if you want to, and if it serves you.

A few things you should know: You can want to quit drinking and not be able to yet. You can quit drinking and start again and want to quit again. You can try to moderate, realize it's not working, and try again. You can keep drinking and just follow the curiosity that led you to pick up this book and let that be enough for now.

This is not about long-term commitment or perfection.

Just be sure to invite God into it with you, knowing he's the best partner to have.

ROCK BOTTOM IS NOT A LOCATION

We often hear that someone must hit "rock bottom" before they're willing to change. That may be true for some people, but it's not a rule! Rock bottom is an elusive concept, and reaching the absolute worst day of one's life isn't a prerequisite for substantive life change. When we hear that someone hit rock bottom, we might imagine her drunk and passed out on the street, getting arrested for disorderly conduct, or maybe leaving her children unattended.

But what if "rock bottom" was missing a deadline? Forgetting to change a kid's wet diaper? Snapping at your husband unnecessarily? Waking up with insomnia at three in the morning most nights?

As Christians, we aren't immune to disastrous or diminutive consequences of alcohol abuse. The numbers regarding women worldwide are mirrored inside the church walls. In 2023, according to the National Institute on Alcohol Abuse and Alcoholism (NIAAA), around 9 percent of adult women in the US struggled with alcoholism—about 11.7 million women. This means that in an average church of five hundred people, at least twenty women attending likely struggle with alcohol dependence as well.

If you add in women who might admit to being uncomfortable with their relationship with alcohol, it's far more. This discomfort, often called "gray-area drinking," is the kind of hush-hush thing women google on incognito mode in the middle of the night. Gray-area drinkers (defined as those who drink more than they'd like to) might identify with the term "high-bottom" or "high-functioning" drinker. We're up at five in the morning, chugging water, reading our Bibles, working out, arriving to work on time, making dinner, shuttling kids to ball games, and volunteering in the nursery at church.

Still, drinking is an issue we can't shake, no matter how deeply we felt the Spirit during the worship band's rendition of "How Great Is Our God." During the song, we feel empowered to overcome. Later that afternoon, the reality of home projects, whiney kids, the Sunday scaries, or some other looming issue overwhelms us, and we think, "Just a little relief would help me through this." And whether you just have a little, or drain the full bottle, the feeling of weakness, codependence and frustration is the same for us all. The world says it's fine to do this every so often, but I'd encourage you to consider the question in your life and your personal consequence. Maybe this kind of drinking isn't fine for you if it cultivates regretful, conflicting emotions.

NIAAA reports that 25 percent of women admit to binge drinking in the last month, or consuming four or more drinks in two hours. With numbers like that, it's easy to justify binge drinking as normal. Still, everyone's experience is different, since alcohol consumption is highly affected by body chemistry, weight, food, energy, and mental state.

It's far too easy to rely on these technical definitions to avoid admitting the problem. Four drinks is subjective, depending on whether we're pouring a standard-sized drink. Rarely is one person's glass of wine only four ounces. Let's be honest: It's not about the quantity now, but the reason behind the drinking in the first place.

The choice is before you. The only thing "bottom" means is that you've had enough of this. You're not a stereotype, but what direction does drinking move you toward? And what direction does *not* drinking move you?

Rock bottom, high bottom—you decide when things aren't working anymore. I didn't want to see how bad it *could* get. I didn't want to get a DUI, embarrass myself in front of colleagues, or blow up my life because of a momentary decision made while drunk. As the mother of a one-year-old back then, I imagined what could happen to her if I lost focus for even a moment. She could crawl away, choke on something, get lost, or hurt. I felt a searing conviction to ensure I kept both of my children safe from the potential consequences of a drunken mom.

I once read a story that really scared me. A woman described her "rock-bottom" moment. She'd decided to have afternoon drinks with a new neighbor who was also a mom to young kids. After a few hours next door, the writer of the story put her baby to bed. By this time, fully buzzed and craving more alcohol, she continued drinking with the neighbor. Her next memory was waking up inside her neighbor's house on the floor, having blacked out. She collected her thoughts, and panic set in as she remembered she'd left her baby napping in the crib. With a hammering headache, she ran out of the front door and back to her own house, where her husband was holding their baby with a look of disgust on his face. He'd come home to find the baby crying and his wife nowhere in sight . . . hours before.

That story may sound foreign, unlike something you'd ever imagine doing. I couldn't see that happening to me either, but every time I drank my defenses were down. Nothing so dire had ever happened to me as a mother. But a sickening feeling crept up on me as I realized that by overdrinking, I opened myself up to tragic possibilities. For my children, it wasn't just their physical safety at risk, but *their* potential future struggles. With addiction genes strong on both sides of our families, my kids are more prone to alcohol abuse than the average person.

For that reason, and plenty more, I knew my best prevention effort would be to quit drinking. That may be a drastic move for some, but for me, it was just one more incentive to kick something toxic out of my home and my life. We don't keep alcohol in the house and, outside of when they were really small, they've never seen their mom intoxicated.

The thing is, kids are perceptive. Even babies know immediately when you are not yourself. You're not fooling anyone, least of all them.

For me, there were also blackouts. Not everyone who drinks blacks out, but I had a history. I didn't black out often, and largely avoided them after having kids. But I'd experienced them often enough to leave gaps in my memory—entire nights erased, with only the vague sense that something wasn't right. To this day, how I got home in some instances remains a mystery.

(As a side note: My own drinking habits did shift during parenthood. I don't mention this as a judgment on anybody else, but because I think it's helpful to share these kinds of details. After becoming a parent, I drank more frequently, but not in the same large amounts as I once did.)

HIGH-FUNCTIONING WOMEN

Have you ever excused your drinking because no one else noticed how bad things were? Maybe no one has ever spoken to you about your drinking, so you couldn't have a real problem, right? High-functioning drinkers often wait for an external sign to tell them it's time to change. All the while, they ignore the emotional misery of shame and fear that consumes them.

This isn't just about how much or how often you drink—it's about the posture of your heart. As Christians, we are freed from the law's burden, but we're still called to keep our hearts aligned with God. After his own confrontation with sin, David asked God to give him a "clean heart" and "renew a right spirit" within him (Psalm 51:10).

If you're convicted that drinking muddies your heart and what comes of it corrupts the Spirit's work, you can and should make the same request David did. I wrongly relied on the opinions of others to assess how problematic things were for too long. I'm not alone.

On the *Tamron Hall Show*, Pastor Irene Rollins shared a relatable story. She was a high-functioning drinker who led a church with her husband outside of Baltimore. A mother of three and spiritual shepherd to thousands, she said she'd "rather die" than have congregants and other loved ones learn about her secret alcohol addiction. At the time, she didn't even have a name for her struggle. She only felt the shame would be too overwhelming if others discovered it.

Plus, she'd been maintaining her secret drinking for so many years that such dysfunction felt "normal"—a daily pathway so worn it felt impossible to dig out of the deep grooves she'd tread. "I felt shame about the fact that I was a pastor and a leader and a mom," she said. "Shame . . . says 'I am bad and I am broken' and 'I am unfixable,' so the very gospel that says I'm forgiven and freed—I didn't believe it myself."

There's the spiritual element of addiction, harnessed by Satan, who asks you, "Did God *really* say that?"

Did he really say *all* your sins are forgiven?

Did he really say we can do *all* things through Christ?

Did he really say *all* believers have been set free?

Satan likes to twist Scripture and use it against us. And when we drink, we actually open ourselves up to more of his lies. We *invite* him in. The world, including Satan, Big Alcohol, and your local mom's group, wants women to believe that drinking alcohol is no big deal. If that's true, what makes us question it?

Ultimately, Irene stepped out in faith and into a rehab program. She believed that God would use her story for good and that the God she proclaimed on the stage would walk with her in the valley and shelter her by the shade of his wings. She trusted Scripture, which promised God was an "ever-present help" (Psalm 46:1 NIV), even when she didn't *feel* it. She recovered and began to share her story as an empowerment tool for others.

God's truth is greater than the emotionally laden fiction we tell ourselves about why we need alcohol. I finally figured it out. So did Irene—and thousands of other women just like you. Freedom is closer than you think.

WEIGHING YOUR FAITH

Despite what you may have heard, a stronger faith isn't the solution here. It's tempting to think that if we were better Christians, we wouldn't turn to alcohol or battle anxiety and depression. But faith isn't the problem—or the cure. Addiction isn't a measure of belief; it's influenced by genetics, environment, life experiences, and culture. This understanding can bring us healing.

It's easy to inadvertently see faith as an action driven by will. This flawed perspective shifts the burden onto us. But the good news is that we can put our trust in God during these challenging times. It's not all on us.

In these weak moments, we don't have to bear the burden—if we *allow* it, he will come through. "He gives power to the faint, and to him who has no might he increases strength" (Isaiah 40:29).

For many of us, the origins of this burden go back to childhood. We were still becoming who we would be, finding our faith, and working through everything that comes with adolescence. For me, like many women, my addiction issues didn't begin with alcohol. It's not uncommon for women who dealt with eating disorders, like I did, to transition into substance abuse—or tack it on. In the *International Journal of Eating Disorders*, researchers Fares Qeadan and Kevin English found that college students with eating disorders were "significantly more likely" to have substance use issues.

All of these addictive, self-sabotaging behaviors are deeply connected. They're rooted in the human heart, shaped by the shame, inadequacy, and fear first sown in the Garden. After Adam and Eve sinned, they felt exposed and ashamed, instinctively covering themselves, hiding, and trying to compensate for their short-comings. Humanity has been doing the same ever since in big and small ways.

As a naive teenager with a newly budding faith, I thought the main issue was my lack of faith, that I wasn't a strong enough Christian. If I could power through these feelings of lack, I would soar. That mindset plagued me for more than a decade. Trusted leaders and self-help books had told me that feelings weren't trustworthy and that, through Christ, we had power over them. There's some truth in this narrative. But you don't "take your thoughts captive" by pretending they don't exist and hoping they go away.

At nineteen, when my therapist recommended antidepressants, I rejected the idea. I thought Christians shouldn't need a pill to give them joy. Eventually, my therapist convinced me that I needed medicine for my sickness—and there was nothing wrong with my faith for that. Just as one takes insulin for diabetes or chemotherapy for cancer, I needed antidepressants to treat my depression and anxiety. If you've never thought of your struggle this way, consider it. It can powerfully alter your perspective and offer self-compassion. Even if you're not sure what you need, thinking this way can give you permission to ask questions and access resources. Remaining open to possible solutions is freeing.

Taking medication or receiving therapy doesn't mean your recovery is divorced from faith. As Christians, our faith practices are essential for overcoming all challenges. However, the divide between spiritual and secular tools of recovery is artificial and arbitrary. Secular resources like support groups, books, podcasts, and meditation can all be used for God's glory and our spiritual benefit. It's the intention behind how we use most tools that flavors the results. That said, I do think that believers are best served by communing and engaging with like-minded Christians as much as we can.

Christ alone is our Savior, but he's provided many tools, people, and pathways to recovery with him. Imagine not one lone rope swinging down from heaven, but an entire web beneath it, extending as widely as necessary to offer footholds and safe havens. That's what it can be like when we employ the supports around us.

IMAGINING THE OTHER SIDE

You might wish you could stop wanting to drink, or at least erase the guilt around it—especially when you don't fully understand why it's there. Why do we turn to alcohol, even when it doesn't align with our faith or sense of self? The faint pencil lines of faded prayers in bedside journals tell the story of my struggle just a few years ago. In these pages, I'm pleading with God to remove my desire to drink.

What I know now: I didn't stop wanting to drink *then*. But ultimately, I stopped wanting to hide.

I began to wonder what my life would be like if I allowed God to sanctify me through the pain of detaching from my idol of alcohol. I imagined that there might be something better on the other side of alcohol, and I knew I couldn't find out if I stayed where I was.

Everyone is allowed on to the other side of alcohol, but it takes hard work to get there. That requires continued curiosity and honesty about alcohol in your life. In my most profound days of struggle, I asked myself a pivotal question: Do you want to be praying about this same problem when you're seventy-five? I did not. And I knew the only way I would not be doing so was if I took my desire to kick alcohol seriously.

Imagine a life free from alcohol—without the questioning and doubt about its place.

Imagine having the capacity to work through *other* things, those you've put on hold since alcohol sucked all the air out of the room.

Imagine the brain space, time replacement, and the ability to focus on *different* concerns more fully.

Satan would have us believe this problem isn't a big deal—or that admitting it would bury us in shame. His lies are personal, tailored to keep us trapped. He'd love to keep us exactly where we are—unable to function fully in freedom.

When Pastor Irene finally dealt with her drinking problem, she said it was like standing in front of her congregation for the first time "as myself." It was scary and vulnerable, but when she looked into the audience, she received only empathy and love from the crowd. Because of that, *everything* changed.

We think judgment is coming. But it's love that returns.

"We [have] normalized recovery in our church . . . so many people got helped, healed, set free," she said. "When we share our story, we're saying that what God did for me, he can do again for you."

Shame will tell you to hide, but the truth will free you.

PAUSE & ASSESS

Documenting questions and new knowledge about alcohol is helpful in assessing things accurately. As you continue reading and analyzing your relationship with alcohol, write down those observations in a journal or app.

I recommend starting a blank Google document or fresh notebook to record insights and answers.

You may start by asking yourself these questions:

- ☐ What first compelled you to drink alcohol?
- ☐ What problem were you trying to solve?
- ☐ Why do you feel guilty or moved to investigate this in the first place?
- ☐ What's your family history with substance abuse?
- ☐ What relevant trauma have you experienced?

In approaching these questions, record anything that comes to mind. When we can identify the root of the desire to drink, it's easier to understand it—and cultivate next steps.

More things you might record in your journal:

- ☐ Questions you're asking
- ☐ Revelations that appear
- ☐ Significant memories
- ☐ Relevant Bible verses
- ☐ What you're hearing from God
- ☐ Helpful thoughts or conversations
- ☐ Prayers you pray
- ☐ Frustrations that arise
- ☐ Any confusion or friction that appears

FOUR

THE SOCIAL DILEMMA

FOR MOST, DRINKING BEGINS as a social activity—for fun, celebration, and social lubrication. Often, it can turn into dependence, with self-medication as the norm.

A familiar joke among women is that book clubs are just wine clubs in disguise. Whether or not the book gets read is beside the point. I've joined my share of wine—oops, I mean *book*—clubs over the years—though I appreciate that many of my fellow members both read the books and consumed the wine! For years, I looked forward to book club, mainly because it was a free pass to drink in peace. Even on Mondays, the wine flowed. Since everyone in my book club was also a member of my church, there was no question to me that this was fine.

In my twenties, it was common for church friends to mix drinking activities with small group gatherings, leaving me confused in both my head and heart. No one seemed to consider that alcohol might be a stumbling block for a fellow sister in Christ. I wouldn't have admitted it even if someone had asked, but I notice it's rarely something people think about.

Social anxiety frazzled my nerves; wine settled them. As a kid, I was so terrified of awkward silences on the phone that I'd write out a list of at least ten conversation topics beforehand—just to make sure I never ran out of things to say.

If invited to a friend's house, I would agonize over what might happen if we ran out of things to do or discuss. Were these the signs of a budding substance abuser? Perhaps.

Particular personality types are more likely to face dependence on alcohol or drugs. In their blog post "Childhood Stress and Anxiety" fact sheet, the Yale School of Medicine shares that untreated childhood anxiety can result in higher rates of substance abuse in adulthood. Of course, addiction is far more complex than that, but there *are* common personality traits associated with higher substance abuse risk in women. Neuroticism, which is characterized by frequent negative emotions like anxiety, worry, irritability, and self-doubt, is chief among them, according to work by Morten Ellegaard Hell and Anders Müller in *Alcoholism: Clinical and Experimental Research.* In their core resource on alcohol for health care professionals, the National Institutes of Health also highlights strong genetic markers for inherited responses to alcohol, alcohol metabolism, and a variety of other vulnerabilities.

As women, we often use alcohol to mask social fears or perceived inadequacies. Unfortunately, friends, culture, alcohol brands, and even medical professionals sometimes told us drinking was an empowering and healthy way to overcome nerves. I even had a doctor once recommend a glass of wine to relax when I was feeling stressed!

For many years, studies proclaimed the heart-healthy benefits of some kinds of alcohol. In an article on red wine and resveratrol, the Mayo Clinic claims that red wine leads to benefits like prevention of blood clots, lowering of bad cholesterol, and improvements in blood vessel linings. In the 2018 article "Federal Agency Courted Alcohol Industry to Fund Study on Benefits of Moderate Drinking," *The New York Times* investigated the studies that led to these claims. What they found was shocking: The alcohol industry was funding this research. Can you imagine a more damning conflict of interest? Reporter Roni Caryn Rabin reported that five alcohol companies helped fund—and possibly even design—a trial with the National Institute on Alcohol Abuse and Alcoholism (NIAAA). The intent was to answer one question: Does moderate drinking reduce the risk of cardiovascular disease?

Researchers actually persuaded alcohol industry executives to fund the study by claiming it was a rare chance to prove that moderate drinking is not only safe but lowers risks of disease. Makes sense—we all want to believe that alcohol is good for us, because we want to justify its comfort. But while we were being misled, alcohol was poisoning our bodies and growing in our lives. Our insecurities were growing exponentially. And each time we turned to alcohol, life became even harder to manage without a substance.

A SOCIAL DRINKING CULTURE

Drinking culture differs across various stages of American life. It can begin in high school, roll into college, continue into young professional life, and ultimately, for women, into so-called mommy wine culture. Drinking doesn't always come to a natural end; there's always another reason to extend the drinking life.

Because drinking is so commonly paired with celebrations—weddings, vacations, parties—there's also a false idea that this kind of happy drinking is risk-averse. But consider that when we drink in celebration, our brains associate alcohol with happiness and good memories. So when stress or anxiety hits, we try to recreate that initial good feeling. But without the original context of our drinking—the people, event, or celebration—that feeling is distorted. But still, we remember when it felt terrific; we continue trying to recreate that same essence. All the while, we suffer from the long-term effects of alcohol use. In the *British Medical Journal*, researchers Anya Topiwala and Charlotte Allan measured hippocampal atrophy, gray matter density, and white matter microstructure in drinkers. They found these drinkers had a notable cognitive decline over time.

It's a sad, self-perpetuating cycle of self-medication and disappointment. Alcohol's assurances consistently deliver empty promises: relief from stress, a sense of companionship, social acceptance, and the illusion of feeling "normal" when things are out of whack. But such promises are so short-lived we feel robbed before the night even ends. And worse, drinking with others often strains relationships. Friends can disappear as quickly as the drink in your hand. The trouble is that none of us consciously decided to become this person. For me, it was hard to pinpoint when my reliance on alcohol clicked from casual to compulsory— when it slid from normal to concerning.

I initially chalked my heavy drinking up to my lack of a rebellious phase in high school. College gave me the opportunity to finally fit in. Then, it felt like drinking went from optional to required, and meeting new people was directly affiliated with consumption. "In college, we can wear our alcohol abuse as proudly as our university sweatshirts; the two concepts are virtually synonymous," writes Koren Zailckas in her book *Smashed*. That's how it felt for me, and the trend continues.

NIAAA found that 28 percent of college students admit to binge drinking in the last month, and 13 percent meet the criteria for alcohol use disorder.

How many of those kids at the bars with me also attended church on Sundays and Christian student meetings on Thursdays? If I was any indication, the number was too high. I wouldn't give up my faith *or* the alcohol. I pushed the convicting thoughts to the back of my mind, but quietly told myself: You can't live this double life forever.

Beyond using alcohol as an ego booster, I also used it to quiet my perpetually stimulated brain and enhance friendships. I learned to perceive drinking together as equivalent to bonding. So many fun nights were infused with cocktails and wine bottles. My friends and I thought alcohol was an essential element of the experience. I was convinced that alcohol temporarily sparked life into what I thought were the best parts of me—that I wouldn't be likable without it.

Drinking to inebriation, and the associated hangover the next day, were a regular part of the fun. We passed around memes: "Here's to nights we'll never remember with friends we'll never forget." Honestly, though? There's nothing funny about forgetting your entire night.

After college, alcohol's lure continues. Building connections in adulthood is more complicated, so the convenient solution of drinking helps us navigate those awkward early interactions. The buzz of a hoppy beverage can enhance a shared interest in books, or the similar ages of kids. We feel instantly relaxed, able to shut off the tabs in our brain set on work deadlines, a kid's medical issue, or our lingering marital problem. As an adult, I couldn't imagine not having the crutch I'd first leaned on at sixteen with a sip of Boone's Farm strawberry wine.

The earlier one drinks, the more likely they'll face addiction. The NIAAA reports that alcohol abuse during adolescence "has been linked to changes within and between brain regions." Moreover, heavy drinking "weakens connections between brain areas that regulate emotional and cognitive functioning." Delaying the first use of alcohol or drugs significantly reduces the chances of addiction, according to research from Mass General Brigham. In later adulthood, the brain has matured and established pathways that better mitigate the risk of addiction; sadly, most people begin abusing substances years before this.

Of course, even if unhealthy drinking begins later in life, it can be harmful or destructive. Drinkers keep drinking because the drink itself isn't the goal—it's the means to an end. We drink because we were told it would help. In the end, it was a lie.

WHEN FUN GOES SOUTH

Because alcohol is so common, recognizing a problem in others is difficult. Some can mask inebriation well. Usually, I could, but not always.

It was summertime at my parents' house, and we'd had a birthday party where alcohol flowed freely. I enjoyed some strongly mixed cocktails, and the atmosphere was light and free—until I went to the basement. It was silent and empty save for a refrigerator full of booze, including a frosty glass handle of vodka. The thrill of being secretly, safely alone to drink it without anyone knowing propelled me forward. My heart raced as if it were some secret, romantic tryst. Before I had kids, which was the case here, it was easy to lose myself in the heat of a moment like this one.

I tipped the bottle back, taking a long swallow. Toxic warmth bloomed from nose to toes, and a dangerous calm settled in. The feeling I'd been pining for—this warm, perfect, happy—arrived. That was one of my last memories of the day.

My next cogent moment was waking in the guest bedroom with a headache, dry mouth, and most painfully, self-hatred. I tried piecing the night together, vaguely recalling an attempt to put my one-year-old nephew to bed as a "favor" to my sister. At some point, she had realized why I couldn't get him down and took over. After that, I'd ghosted everyone, shutting the bedroom door and passing out.

Accusatory questions assaulted my mind that morning. Why had I done this? Why did I *always* do this? What was wrong with me? I collapsed onto the floor and called my husband, who was back in our home state. When he answered, I could barely speak, sobbing that I had let myself drink so much.

"I have to quit drinking," I said. I repeated it, scared of what it meant and sure that I couldn't do it. I dreaded walking out of the bedroom to face my family. When I finally left the room, they just laughed off my "crazy" night. I hadn't done or said anything destructive, so they thought my botched attempt at getting my nephew to bed was hilarious.

"How did you get so drunk?" my sister asked lightheartedly.

I played it off, laughing at myself and telling them I had no idea how that happened. But I *knew*. Secrecy and lies are telltale. Question yourself when these behaviors become common. A nonabusive drinker doesn't think like an alcoholic, so my sister didn't fathom that I might have been sneaking extra sips of vodka when no one was looking.

I managed a hangover all day, gulping down tall glasses of cold water, popping Excedrin pills, and drinking electrolytes. I hesitated to turn to God in my despair. How could I face him with this? I'd done it to myself. Why should he have any sympathy?

Random pieces of Scripture played like a mixed tape as I pitied my bad choices:

- "No temptation has overtaken you." (1 Corinthians 10:13)
- "Rejoice always." (1 Thessalonians 5:16)
- "I can do all things through him who strengthens me." (Philippians 4:13)
- "Do not be conformed to this world." (Romans 12:2)
- "Your enemy the devil prowls around like a roaring lion looking for someone to devour." (1 Peter 5:8 NIV)

I answered each Scripture passage:

- But God, temptation overtook me.
- But God, joy didn't appear.
- But God, I could barely get out of bed.
- But God, I had been fully conformed to the world.
- But God, the devil had easily and quickly devoured me.

What kind of Christian—one that was writing faith-based books and articles and teaching Sunday school—had such a limited faith and destructive behavior? The thoughts went round and round.

By evening, my wounds were bandaged. Less than eight hours after vowing to quit, I craved the high-alcohol IPAs my dad kept stocked in the garage. The life-sucking cycle continued.

My body had succumbed to the craving patterns—to function, survive, and numb the shame. Once my mind and body ordered the emotional pain to leave, I felt powerless to resist what it took to make that happen. Compulsion was ruthless. I could look in the mirror and watch the theoretical control I had melt in the face of a craving.

DRINKING MOMS

In motherhood, things can get worse. Mothers of young children are frequently encouraged to unwind with a deserved glass of wine or cocktail. Folks may think it's kind to issue a guilt-free pass like this, but it can lead some women down a dark road.

Author Stefanie Wilder-Taylor cultivated online fame through her "wine mom" persona, even writing bestselling books like *Naptime Is the New Happy Hour*, a book about the realities of motherhood. Though she didn't explicitly tell women to drink, the book celebrated drinking as a coping mechanism. Years later, she got sober after realizing how problematic her drinking had become.

In an ABC News piece, "If Sobriety Has Taught Me Anything," she wrote:

> I am just like you. Maybe I drank more or maybe I drank less, but I was just a mom you may have passed at the grocery store buying frozen waffles, or playing with my kids on the lawn in the summer.
>
> I wasn't on skid row or working on a novel from my jail cell. I've never had a DUI or been drunk before 9:00 a.m. but I'm still an alcoholic. I always think that maybe, if more women had been out in the open, I could have seen myself more clearly and not been embarrassed to ask for help.

There is immense pressure to embrace drinking as a social, mental, and professional stress reliever. The popularity of mommy wine culture persists, creating a challenging environment for women who genuinely want to break free.

Walking around with your kids on Halloween? Take a roadie.

Biding your time at a trampoline park? Grab a beer at the bar.

Playdate on a Saturday afternoon? It's the weekend—*of course* we're drinking!

Alcohol is sold at the zoo, the jump park, the family Christmas festival, and the Harvest Fair.

"Alcohol's been sold as the ultimate way to decompress, to cope, and to bond with other women. And it's very dangerous," says Ann Dowsett Johnson, author of *Drink: The Intimate Relationship Between Women and Alcohol.* She tells Christian Broadcasting Network News that decades ago, it was "practically unheard of" for moms to drink together while caring for their children. But, alcohol marketing changed all that. If you don't drink, someone might tell you to "lighten up" or embrace motherhood's monotony with friends who carry Stanley cups brimming with vodka and electrolytes.

We can't blame all our problems on marketing, but it's valid to identify the sneaky tactics behind them.

DRINKING CHRISTIANS

Barna research reveals that 60 percent of practicing Christians drink alcohol, and 30 percent of those who drink say they sometimes have "more than they should." This second category is ambiguous, varying in both scope and interpretation. Lifeway surveys from 2018 show that Christians generally drink less than their secular peers, but substance abuse doesn't discriminate. The church has a long way to go in ministering to women in this category. Christian women are swayed by cultural shifts, and advertising too.

The question remains: How much is too much? Alcohol consumption *is* acceptable in many Christian circles, but to what end? In many ways, we've lost a once-widespread fear of appearing legalistic or prudish. It may sound superficial, but it's taken many years for Christians to shed these labels.

In recent years, Christians have shunned the hard boundaries of teetotaling fundamentalism, preferring not to be labeled "legalistic." For example, places like Moody Bible College lifted their alcohol ban. As reported by *Christianity Today*, Moody spokesperson Brian Regnerus said the change "came out of a desire in Moody's leadership to reflect a high-trust environment that emphasizes values, not rules," and to "require no more and no less than what God's Word requires."

This combination of factors meant even church ladies and stay-at-home moms joined the ranks of those tipping back more frequently. It's easy to fall into a struggle with alcohol, yet hard to admit it when things get messy.

Even Christian friends can unknowingly contribute to the problem. Two of mine, at one point, discussed a particularly stressful day one of them had experienced. In a lighthearted tone, the other said, "Oooh, you need a margarita!"

The unquestioned message is pervasive: we both need and deserve alcohol for our stress, parenting, or work.

Using alcohol as self-medication undermines any other potential remedy for relief and distances us from God. The relaxation or peace we crave may emerge temporarily, but ultimately, alcohol makes it harder to achieve these states naturally.

In a Cleveland Clinic article, "Anxiety and Alcohol," researchers note that alcohol is both a sedative and a depressant. "It can relieve feelings of fear or anxiety in the moment," they write. "But after the alcohol wears off, you can start to feel your anxiety come back even stronger."

That's what poisons do: infiltrate healthy places and intoxicate them, making it much harder to achieve strength and vitality.

WHERE'S THE LINE BETWEEN SOCIAL DRINKING AND PROBLEM DRINKING?

Today, we are more aware of problematic drinking scenarios in media, advertising, and jokes than ever. However, knowledge doesn't necessarily make it easier to change behavior—partly because we're unsure what's actually "problematic."

How do we move from fun and social to dangerous and sinful? Is there a moment or a subtle shift? Each person is different, but when it comes to social drinkers vs. alcoholics, here are a few ways to distinguish between the two:

- A social drinker *only* drinks in social settings and is not interested in drinking alone or drinking excessively.

- A social drinker can easily stop drinking for any reason. An alcoholic has trouble saying no, even with a good reason, such as a pending early morning, driving responsibilities, or professional etiquette.

- A social drinker may be affected by one or two drinks, while an alcoholic's high tolerance often requires more drinks to feel the effects.

- A social drinker can choose not to drink at an event, but an alcoholic may be hyperfocused on the alcohol and is rarely able to refrain from drinking if it's present.
- A social drinker can drink without getting drunk, while an alcoholic may feel powerless to stop drinking before significant intoxication.
- A social drinker doesn't usually have hangovers, health complications, or suffer in work or family life because of their drinking.
- A social drinker doesn't feel guilt, shame, or regret after drinking, but an alcoholic frequently does.

Each person must evaluate their own relationship with alcohol. Just because something doesn't rise to the level of concern for others doesn't mean it's not a personal or spiritual issue for you. Furthermore, social drinking without issues doesn't erase the times when drinking *is* destructive. At times it's difficult to know which way it will turn out when the night begins.

I was jealous of those who could volunteer to drive or have only a few drinks. I wondered how my sister could go out with friends, keep her drinking in check, and wake up somewhat refreshed the next day. She switches to water between drinks and knows her limits. I longed for that self-control and ability to have fun within boundaries.

The way I romanticized drinking, as many do, didn't help. The first sip was almost poetic, my cells vibrating with a happy hum. The crescendo of that feeling matched the pace of a chilled wine dripping like an IV into my bloodstream. In an instant, the world was brighter and lighter. I knew that regret, pain, and shame would quash all that when the booze wore off, but for now? Now was all that mattered.

Using alcohol to soothe a hard day, ice out a moment, or hack through a relational issue only amplifies that problem later in one way or another. Cultural norms prompt us to block out messages that our brains, bodies, and hearts know to be true: alcohol is not what's best for us.

As I mentioned previously, we've unintentionally trained our bodies to think they need alcohol. Understanding this is imperative. Once we cognitively know that this mind message is a ruse, we can change the message. The Recovery Research Institute suggests that therapeutic interventions and sobriety can work in tandem to change the brain and reduce "neural cue reactivity," which is what causes one to crave alcohol ("Retrain the Brain: Effects on Neural Alcohol Cue Reactivity").

As hard as it is to quit drinking or end any bad habit, God made our bodies brilliantly and resiliently.

WHAT ALCOHOL DEPENDENCE ISN'T

Misuse of alcohol isn't the caricature we often see in movies or books. It doesn't always—or usually—look like a man pushing a rusted shopping cart down a crumbling sidewalk or a woman making a sloppy scene at the holiday staff party.

It's the woman who shows up to the six o'clock morning yoga class sweating out the toxins from her nightly bottle of wine. It's the mom who manages class parties and chaperones field trips, secretly plotting what she'll drink when she gets home. Alcohol addiction is hiding in oversized Stanley tumblers at soccer games and a thrice-filled, wide-bottomed wine glass during the hour spent cooking dinner and cleaning it up.

Alcohol doesn't ask anything of us. It says, "Just relax." It's a friend who doesn't ask too many questions and makes you feel so much is possible—tomorrow, of course. It beckons you with false promises you'll later discover are lies. Late actor Matthew Perry, who struggled with drugs and alcohol, wrote in his book, *Friends, Lovers, and the Big Terrible Thing*, that "reality is an acquired taste, and I failed to acquire it." That hits.

It can feel that way, right? Don't we want a reality that's just a tad softer? The constant yearning for more can easily turn into an obsession, or even feel overwhelming as we try to balance the rules around our drinking. The stakes for normalcy move quickly with substances. The body adapts and asks for an unending more.

PAUSE & REFLECT

- When you first drank alcohol, how did you feel about it? How do you feel about it now, and what has changed?
- Can you name a positive experience you associate with alcohol? What else was positive about that experience besides the alcohol?
- Make a list of things you naturally associate with drinking. After looking over your list, do you find it accurate or helpful to pair drinking with these events, moments, or memories?

FIVE

THE SELF-MEDICATION
DELUSION

IN THE MOVIE *Flight*, Denzel Washington plays an alcoholic pilot so skilled that when disaster hits midair, he lands the plane successfully, avoiding disaster. Later, we find out he had alcohol in his system when it happened, and legal chaos ensues.

The night before the verdict, in a hotel room alone, he finds the door to an empty, connected room with a stocked minibar. My heart breaks for him in this scene; he feels completely powerless to resist the call of a drunken escape.

The next day, he haphazardly sobers up. He's a master of disguise who has maintained professional appearances mid-hangover for years, so no one is the wiser. It appears he will win the case, get off scot-free, and walk away a hero.

But on the stand, he cracks, unable to live with one more lie. He admits that he was drunk, that he's drunk "right now," and needs help. He finally recognizes that the only way out of this prison is through authentic confession. Denzel's character emanates light as the weight of secrecy rises from his shoulders. He even smiles. This man is a talented and skilled pilot who has done his job well. He is also an alcoholic. Two things of this nature can coexist without one diminishing the other.

What makes someone like Denzel's character do this? Why would this successful, accomplished, and respected man make such risky choices to feed his addiction? Well, it had just become a way of life. He relied on it to get through each day, as the numbing power of substances stripped away his ability to discern or care, whether for himself or anyone else. It was self-medication.

When we drink, we're not necessarily being bad. We *are* trying to fix our pain, or meet a need in a moment where relief seems priceless. Issues may include:

- Depression
- Anxiety or fear (avoidance)
- Self-esteem or confidence
- Not-enoughness, or shame
- Loneliness (need for companionship)
- Grief
- Boredom
- Lack of control
- Lack of love
- Stress
- Unhealed trauma

Self-medicating to feel better makes sense on its face. With each discomfort, hardship, or resistance, we prescribe ourselves the remedy of alcohol. But we're not doctors—and there's no check in, oversight, or follow-up appointment on deck.

To say "life is hard"—when we have it pretty good compared to the rest of the world—can be guilt-inducing. When I start feeling sorry for myself, I immediately conjure images of displaced refugee families, starving Somali children, or those living under the oppression of the North Korean government. Compared to these, I've got nothing to complain about.

But there are things in my life that are hard. Even if you think they *shouldn't* be hard—they just are. And we must reckon with this, accept that hard is relative, and believe that that's okay. Stress, isolation, trauma, social anxiety, parenthood, and work can all be difficult to manage at times. If not properly addressed, our hardships trigger our mind and body to respond with desire.

And contrary to popular belief, alcohol is a serious drug. We don't take psychiatric drugs without the consultation of a doctor (at least, we're not supposed to) because they can bring serious consequences if abused or if you experience side effects. We need to treat alcoholic self-medication with the same seriousness. Legalization has led us to believe it's simply a beverage; it's not.

No one was checking on Denzel. No one was checking on me. No one's been checking on you. It's time to make an appointment for yourself.

WHEN YOU WANT TO SELF-MEDICATE

Relying on substances means that surviving without them seems impossible. In *The American Journal of Medicine*, researchers Alexandra Matarazzo and Charles Hennekens report that deaths from alcohol among women have doubled in the last ten years. In fact, the number of deaths from alcohol overall has doubled in the last twenty years, with deaths in women increasing two and a half times.

The anxiety-alcohol cycle is vicious: Anxiety is a result of alcohol, and alcohol is a cure for the anxiety. And on it goes. This phenomenon has the unofficial name of "hangxiety." Hangxiety is caused, in part, by chemical changes in our brains when coming down from drinking. The Alcohol and Drug Foundation defines it like this:

> Alcohol works on the brain's GABA (gamma-aminobutyric acid) receptor—this is what makes you feel more relaxed when you start drinking.
>
> As drinking continues, our brains also start to shut off glutamate (which makes you anxious), increasing feelings of calm and being uninhibited.
>
> But as alcohol starts to wear off, our brain tries to restore the normal chemical balance.
>
> It does this by both reducing the brain's GABA (lessening calm feelings) and increasing glutamate (making us feel more anxious). Together this has the opposite effect compared to when you were drinking and increases anxiety.

Some people experience postdrinking anxiety more intensely than others, but those who already struggle with anxiety in daily life are especially prone to its effects—and Big Alcohol has cashed in on this. Until recent decades, alcohol brands marketed themselves primarily to men, emphasizing images of dark, frosty beers ready after a long day of work or playing up the sweet burn of Scotch as an emblem of refined masculinity. In the 1990s, however, the industry recognized women as an undertapped market.

In an interview with WHYY radio, David Jernigan, director of the Center on Alcohol Marketing and Youth at Johns Hopkins University, notes that this increase began with the introduction of sugary drinks for "entry-level" drinkers. A decade later, "skinny" versions of premade cocktails launched for women who wanted low-calorie options. Rates of alcohol use disorder rose by 83 percent between 2002 and 2013, in tandem with the rise in feminized alcohol marketing. Maybe you've noticed the bright, fruity spreads of perky alcoholic beverages stocked in the front display of Target; that's not an accident. Marketers have carefully angled them into your vision upon arrival. Check out the liquor aisle these days, and you'll find a rainbow of cocktails with feminine flavors fashioned to appeal to female empowerment tropes.

In addition to clever marketing, the pace of modern life has accelerated drinking among women. Until the last fifty years or so, most young mothers stayed at home with their children and spent more time together with their children. There was more time for friends, family, and leisure. Today, our lives are commandeered by sports, activities, and scheduled and regulated events. We're not used to unstructured hangouts, so when we enter those spaces, we feel awkward and uncomfortable. And if there's wine available, well, checkmate.

The Wall Street Journal's Sumathi Reddy reports that binge drinking is on the rise among middle-aged women. While men are still more likely to overdrink, the number of women aged thirty-five to fifty who drink binge drink (remember, that means having five or more drinks in a row in a two-week period) has increased nearly twice as fast as men's between 2012 and 2022, according to the University of Michigan's 2022 *Monitoring the Future* report.

Peeking behind the curtain at the real people represented by the numbers is helpful. A woman who attends my online sobriety meetings recently shared something that smacked me right out of my multitasking. She was thirty days out from a DUI, fired from her job, and on probation. She broke down as she told a Zoom room full of strangers about her two children, both with a fatal genetic condition, who had died as toddlers. The grief had led her to excessive drinking, which had since ruined much of the rest of her life. Can you blame her for turning to alcohol? No way. But it became clear that alcohol wasn't the answer. Instead, it had let her down time and again.

AN ISSUE OF CHARACTER (OR IS IT?)

For that woman in my meeting, drinking certainly wasn't an issue of character.

Spitefulness. Pettiness. Dishonesty. Arrogance. Laziness. Cruelty. These words describe traits of "weak" character—the kind of moral failure that comes when one knows the right thing to do but chooses the wrong thing anyway. Feeling oppressed by a substance or behavior doesn't disappear naturally. We must stop beating ourselves up and seek out a path to freedom.

While it's not a moral issue, addiction *is* a lot of other things: physical, mental, and spiritual. It must be dealt with accordingly. In the article "Biology of Addiction," the NIH notes that "much of addiction's power lies in its ability to hijack and even destroy key brain regions that are meant to help us survive." In other words, destructive forces have taken over the brain, making it harder to process decisions rationally.

Northwestern Medicine explains in a blog post titled "How Alcohol Impacts the Brain," "Your whole body absorbs alcohol, but it really takes its toll on the brain. Alcohol interferes with the brain's communication pathways. It can also affect how your brain processes information." And a team of researchers in *Molecular Psychiatry* find that drinking alcohol during high-stakes moments confuse your brain's pleasure and reward circuits, leading the body to believe it needs alcohol to survive difficult times.

The more you repeat this cycle, the more ingrained it becomes, often damaging your essential decision-making abilities. The physical embodiment is overpowering. In these moments, we're not dealing with weak character or moral failings but with a will to live. Our bodies don't know the difference, even if our rational minds do. We walked into our drinking with no comprehension of how difficult it would be to walk away. We believed those who said it was safe, that we deserved it, that it was just to relax, that it's just for fun, that people *like us* don't have problems like *that*.

FEMINIZATION OF ADDICTION

Data tells the story of women and their particular vulnerability to substance abuse: Professionally, women take 69 percent of mental-health-related leaves of absence, and they have twice the rate of generalized anxiety disorder as men.

The feminization of addiction is not new. More than a century ago, male doctors often recommended laudanum, an opiate, to women struggling with anxiety—as if numbing out could solve a more profound, internal issue. In the late 1800s, notes a blog post from *Nursing Clio*, addiction rates among middle-aged, middle- and upper-class women soared. That's the same demographic afflicted by the alcohol epidemic today. In the 1950s, we saw a repeat of this with the barrage of prescriptions for drugs like Valium and Miltown. Around we go again. What were the problems these women had? They're the same ones we have today: dissatisfaction, boredom, depression, repressed emotions, lack of fulfillment, loss of purpose, and more.

Many doctors weren't helping the matter then, and some of them still aren't. For example, my doctor was unaware of my struggle in using alcohol as self-medication, and when I came to him about my anxiety, he recommended I have a glass of wine to unwind. This habit of prescription is alarming. People often lie to doctors about their drinking habits, and they go to extreme lengths to justify their drinking. Suggesting alcohol to medicate is a dangerous tendency.

The root of the problem is a failure to recognize the authentic ailment of the soul, for which alcohol is just self-medication. Unfortunately, yearly written surveys at the doctor's office don't effectively prod our hearts. Without some serious coaxing, most women will continue to bury their genuine emotions and simply carry on. We're women, and we're too busy caring for everyone else's issues to look after our own. If we don't do it, nobody will.

MEDIA LIES

As we've established, the line between drinking as a part of culture and drinking as a crutch is blurry—and it's a spectrum. Rates or chances of dependency or harm are layered. Clear as mud, as they say. Personally, I think that people who don't have a drinking issue don't wonder if they do.

But the media representation of drinking makes it even harder to discern. Old shows like *Sex and the City*, *Mad Men*, and *It's Always Sunny in Philadelphia* feature drinking as a daily habit without adequately showcasing negative consequences like hangovers, addictive potential, weight gain, poor health, or damaged social connections. How many shows or movies have you seen where the main character wakes up late or works the morning after a night out, but looks put together and seems free of a pounding headache? Similarly, how often do you see TV moms tending to toddlers at seven in the morning after a late-night binge? I know from experience that that's not something you *want* to see on TV. I'd lie on the couch with an ice pack on my head, downing Excedrin while praying that my baby would stay content in her bouncer and my toddler would be glad to watch *Paw Patrol* all morning.

A DISEASE TO RECKON WITH

Alcoholism and addiction are diseases of both the mind and body, but they don't fit into our traditional understanding of disease. Unlike most illnesses, ceasing to drink can effectively cure the condition. But alcohol makes quitting incredibly difficult. Once the cycle of addiction begins, the body and brain are fundamentally altered, making it far more difficult to change behaviors. In their bulletin "Biology of Addiction," the NIH reports that drugs and alcohol "hijack" pleasure circuits of the brain, creating what feels like a need for more to function normally. Consider the many people addicted to opiates who aren't taking the drugs for a high, but rather to avoid extreme pain.

Imagery of the brains of addicted people show decreased activity in the prefrontal cortex. In the same bulletin, Nora Volkow of the NIH's National Institute on Drug Abuse says that "people can't make the decision to stop taking the drug—even if they realize the price of taking that drug may be extremely high, and they might lose custody of their children or end up in jail."

Addiction feels like a denial of free will. Again, think about folks who became severely addicted to physician-prescribed opiates without even knowing it, or babies born addicted to heroin—their bodies believe they need drugs to survive. Whose fault was that? Do we think those babies just need to be harder on themselves and practice some self-discipline in order to quit?

We have some similarities with those addicted babies. Yes, we've sinned along the way—but now, part of what we're facing is medical. Our brains have developed a biological dependency on alcohol. It's easy to shame ourselves for slipping up, but addiction has a strong physical and mental pull—and breaking free requires more than just discipline and faith.

In *Addiction and Virtue*, Kent Dunnington tackles the question of whether addiction is a disease or a choice. This controversial question is a hard one to answer. He writes that "addictions are among the most powerful strategies" we have to direct our "most fundamental desires." What are we trying to reach when we drink? As one member of a sobriety community noted, "It finally hit me that I didn't have a problem with alcohol—the problem was I was using alcohol as the solution."

IT'S NOT YOUR FAULT, BUT IT IS YOUR RESPONSIBILITY

Some may bristle at that subhead. For many Christians, it's just a fact that drunkenness is sinful, and that nobody should blame others for their own choices. If you share this background, you might ask: How could addiction not be our fault? If not ours, whose fault could it be?

Let's consider some of the silent factors in our decisions. In a blog post for the Mayo Clinic, Brien Gleeson notes that certain personality types are more vulnerable to dependence on alcohol or drugs. People struggling with addiction often share characteristics like thrill-seeking, risk-taking, and thriving in social environments. People pleasers, empaths, and those with high anxiety, depression, and a history of trauma—such individuals *may* be potential targets for addiction. There may also be a genetic component. Researchers Feng Zhou and William Muir recently identified a group of genes thought to influence alcohol use disorders, publishing their findings in *Alcohol: Clinical and Experimental Research*.

Personality. Genetics. Trauma. Mental Illness. These are things we cannot control, and probably didn't realize were at the root of our drinking.

Yes, sinful choices do play a part in our drinking. We are all sinners living in a fallen world, and this fallenness is ultimately the root of alcoholism. But it's crucial to get beyond the question of sin to consider how and why we often turn to alcohol as a coping mechanism.

Every drinker has a choice. And every one of us *can* overcome our addiction. But it will likely take a more intentional and holistic approach than you may have anticipated. Many a Christian has sat in an AA meeting, repeating that first step that has helped so many reach sobriety: "Admit you are powerless over alcohol." It's controversial, but part of overcoming addiction is the recognizing that alcohol has a particular hold over people—that we can't choose otherwise without God's help. The good news is that even though there's so much that we cannot control, Scripture says that "we are each responsible for our own conduct" (Galatians 6:5 NLT). And so we are here.

Whatever you want to call it—dependence, self-medication—addiction has the power to shake even our strongest foundations. But we need to remember that it is not stronger than the Holy Spirit at work within us. Having named the struggle and begun to understand its roots, we carry the responsibility to act—to pursue healing with the wisdom and clarity we've been given. The reality is that no one can do this for you. But it can be done.

Overcoming may feel impossible. For some, it might sound annoying—perhaps you don't *want* to change your behavior. I get that. I just ask that you continue reading with an open mind and heart for what God wants to reveal. For me, giving up alcohol felt scary and annoying. The thought of giving up alcohol filled me with sadness—not just because of what it had taken from me, but because it had also given me moments that felt meaningful. Not every memory was painful, and that made letting go even harder.

But what about all the bad times? The regret, guilt, nausea, exhaustion, anxiety, and spiritual blockage? Moments I missed with my kids, fights with my husband, poor decisions that could have led to tragedy?

It won't be easy to leave behind ingrained habits and behaviors. Just imagining a different life can feel strange or impossible. But what if you tried it?

That's something I had to ask myself many times when things got bleak. There was that time I drove in a haze to the grocery store. My mind was focused on buying mini wine bottles to gulp down in secret during an anxious night. Then there were the times I'd stuffed tiny bottles into my purse to drink in secret later.

It sure didn't feel, at that time, that I would ever boast of being a month sober, let alone one year.

But against the odds, the impossible slowly became feasible, trackable, and possible. I was encouraged by the thought that millions of people do not drink daily—some because they shouldn't, others because they don't want to. I could join them if I wanted.

Yes, addiction changes the brain, but the brain can change again if we take the right actions. God made our brains malleable that way. In a study in the *New England Journal of Medicine*, the NIH's Nora Volkow writes that "behavior modifications" can "help restore balance in brain circuitry." With the help of science, education, and self-honesty, we can reclaim the power we have in Jesus' name.

WHAT'S NEXT?

Many years ago, when I was pondering the spiritual ethics of using antidepressants, I was ignorant. Today, I have a better theology of mental illness and addiction. That ignorance wasn't my fault, nor was my struggle the result of sin or spiritual weakness. I needed to pursue the kind of health care that addressed the deep issues, which God provided through doctors and medicine. You may need to do the same.

The opposite of self-medicating might be *community* medicating. If you're weaning yourself off drugs, you'll need to be surrounded by others. It's daunting and impossible when we see ourselves floating out in the ether, untethered to anything. Introverts, you're included! With the support and understanding of others, life slowly begins to feel lighter. Unexpected people enter the scene, bringing color, comfort, and a new sense of hope. You meet someone, hear a story, or pray a prayer you never expected—and through these people and moments, God weaves his supernatural work into your life.

We can't discipline ourselves out of addiction. We can't increase our faith enough to "beat" it. But, we can move toward something better with God's guidance, self-compassion, and forgiveness.

PAUSE & REFLECT

- When have you used alcohol to cope with stress, anxiety, or emotional pain?
- Think of a specific time when you turned to alcohol while feeling overwhelmed or disconnected from God. What might this reveal about my current emotional and spiritual health?
- How would your life look if you didn't use alcohol to cope? What healthier coping strategies can you explore?

SIX

SELF-COMPASSION AND FORGIVENESS

WHY DID IT HAVE TO HAPPEN? That was my first thought, displacing blame for taking a drink to anyone or anything that wasn't me. Then again, it *had* felt nearly impossible to say no.

I'd gone through the entire day feeling good, energized, and productive without wanting to drink. I assumed the feeling would continue as the day progressed. But my cravings returned as reliably as the rising sun.

As usual, I dreaded making dinner, so when I saw my neighbors outside with their kids in the afternoon, I avoided cooking. I brought my own children over to play and pushed responsibility out of my mind. As was so often the case, the wine at their house was flowing freely. I often went there, quietly hoping they'd offer me a glass, as they almost always did.

Accepting the glass really didn't feel like a deliberate choice. Wine with friends on a beautiful Tuesday afternoon—that's a very normal thing to do. Normie drinkers do that, and I was definitely normal—at least I tried to be.

I drained the glass within ten minutes. My friend graciously offered a refill. Who was I to refuse? I could get a little buzz, which would help with the dinner dread, and my husband wouldn't even know I'd been drinking. Or I could tell him it had just been a little.

The kids continued playing, and my friend's husband rounded the corner with a glass of bourbon. Immediately, my mouth watered. It was a *horrible* idea. But reason couldn't catch up with desire. I could already taste the fiery bourbon burn, a would-be disinfectant for a busy mind, and I wanted it.

The two glasses of wine had already brought my defenses down. As I guessed he would, my friend's husband poured me a glass of the bourbon. Within an hour, I'd sabotaged my night. One hour of so-called fun. Was it worth it?

Once home, I was brooding with self-hate for decisions I knew had brought this on. I chugged a glass of water, made a pile of cheese quesadillas, and ate until I felt sick. I hoped without hope that the food would soak up the alcohol. *That's it*, I told myself. *I'm quitting drinking tomorrow.*

That conviction remained for about twenty-four hours. (Noticing a pattern yet?) I kept no alcohol at home, as one of my many rules to prevent overdrinking. The next day, I told my husband I needed to run to the store for milk. As I rushed toward the car to leave, I nearly collided with him in my hurry, rabid at the thought of buying a bottle of wine.

Like many trips to the store for wine, this one felt like watching a documentary of myself from the outside. It was someone else reaching for the bottle, pulling out their wallet, smiling at the cashier (surely she was judging), and walking quickly, head down, back to the car. I didn't want to risk stopping for polite conversation. My singular focus was the drug. I just wanted that sparkly feeling of liquid pleasure that would make life tolerable for the night. I revved the engine, irritated by stoplights and drivers with the audacity to go the speed limit. The sooner I could open that bottle, the better.

This robotic routine was rote for me, after years of compulsive habits. It was familiar from nights in college when I binged on cafeteria food alone in my dorm, dreading the early morning runs which I forced myself to do in a futile attempt to burn off the calories. And later, when I lived in Washington, DC, I'd choke down warm vodka from a Capitol Hill liquor store just two blocks from the Supreme Court and half a mile from the White House.

Fifteen years after these awful tendencies had begun in my life, they were still running rampant and worse than ever. I knew there was a better way, but everything seemed pointless compared to a buzz. Yoga, meditation, prayer, exercise—sure, I thought those might help a little, but they were so tame compared to the chemical high of alcohol. That was how my mind operated back then—almost feral when it came to a fix. If you look closely at both people and animals, there's a natural, almost primal instinct to fix what feels off—as fast as possible. Dogs, for instance, lick their wounds to ease pain, triggering the release of the natural painkillers known as endorphins.

For humans, drinking achieves a similar effect. But as we learned in the last chapter, alcohol floods the brain with artificial endorphins, disrupting the balance of our internal reward system. Over time, the brain adapts, demanding ever higher doses for the same fleeting relief. Feeling normal becomes harder; our lows sink lower, and that baseline of normalcy vanishes entirely. We begin chasing the false high, living for the rush. Just as a dog's wound worsens with constant licking, our drinking deepens the damage, compounding the toxicity within us. Animals and humans cope with pain differently, but it's for the same primary reason: When a core need goes unmet, we reach for something to fill the gap. When social, emotional, and spiritual deficiencies overshadow our sense of security, belonging, and purpose, our brains search for anything that will ease our pain. Drinking is simply one method of temporarily meeting our unmet needs.

This is the theology of addiction I wish I had heard in the beginning of my recovery journey. It echoes the truth I mentioned earlier: You can't self-discipline your way out of addiction. You can't pray hard enough or be "spiritual" enough to beat alcohol dependence on your own. That's not because you're weak—it's because life is challenging, and substance reliance is powerful. By grace, Christians are uniquely empowered—not merely by mental or emotional tools but by a spirit made alive through the Holy Spirit (Galatians 5:16).

As Christians, we carry something our secular counterparts don't: a spirit made alive by the Holy Spirit. Recovery isn't just behavior modification—it's soul-level renewal, dealing first with any spiritual roots that may be feeding our addiction, empowered by the Spirit of God within us.

Thankfully, we can implement self-forgiveness, which can help us overcome the enemy's greatest tool: shame. We can do this by applying Scripture and evidence to understand God's perspective, instead of continually relying on our own faulty beliefs.

This theology reminds us that addiction is far deeper than a sinful choice. It's more like being in bondage. Maybe that sounds dramatic to you. But even if you wouldn't describe yourself as a captive, isn't alcohol dependence exhausting? Praise God, Jesus came to set the captives free (Luke 4:18). And we don't have to earn that freedom by perfect behavior or religious effort; instead, we receive it through acceptance, surrender, and grace.

Remember the beautiful words God gave to Paul: "My grace is sufficient for you, for my power is made perfect in weakness" (2 Corinthians 12:9). You might feel weak, as if you've failed. But the gospel assures us that we need not be strong. God's grace is not for some future, better version of you—it's for right now, in your raw, real efforts to make better choices. God sees your desire for change and meets you there in whatever wilderness surrounds you.

Psalm 34:18 reminds us, "The LORD is near to the broken-hearted and saves the crushed in spirit." Being crushed in spirit resonates with me big time. How many times did I disappoint myself? How many times did I end up back at square one? This Bible verse was often my only solace. You and I don't need to prove ourselves to God. He already knows us, loves us, and is committed to our restoration.

Today, I'm able to look at my experience through the lens of mental health and addiction theology. I can better understand Scripture and God's perspective on these matters in my heart, and I can see each step of my journey to today with grace and truth. I want that for you, too. As we learn and grow, this holy, God-centered self-compassion is essential.

THE TRUTH ABOUT ADDICTION AND DEPENDENCE

"For I do not do what I want, but I do the very thing I hate," wrote Paul (Romans 7:15). For me, that may be the most relatable verse in the entire Bible.

Sound familiar?

The verse *after* that one can be a comfort for us, though: "As it is, it is no longer I myself who do it, but it is sin living in me. For I know that good itself does not dwell in me, that is, in my sinful nature. For I have the desire to do what is good, but I cannot carry it out" (Romans 7:17-18 NIV).

We are all born with a sinful nature, unable to overcome it without the grace of Christ. He atoned for every part of our nature, including those elements that feel out of our control. We relieve performance pressure by accepting this fallible nature and believing that any good in us comes from God alone. It's not possible to "do what is good" without God. And while giving everything to God may seem difficult, there's hope in day-to-day, even moment-to-moment, surrender.

In the case of addiction, the "sinful nature" of seeking alcohol has compulsively taken root in the brain. The addicted or dependent brain turns off certain natural functions that must be intentionally retooled to work correctly again. In the grip of addiction or dependence, our brains naturally gloss over painful memories or consequences. Often, our minds deceive us, downplaying the anxiety, hangovers, headaches, and regret, convincing us that the situation isn't that bad or that we don't have a "real" problem. But we need to see through these biased memories and misunderstood myths.

In the video "How an Addicted Brain Works," a Yale Medicine team explains that "addictive substances trigger an outsized response when they reach the brain," which ultimately causes "dopamine to flood the reward pathway, ten times more than a natural reward." I've mentioned this once before, but I want to emphasize again what researchers explain about alcohol and the reward system: "Achieving that pleasurable sensation becomes increasingly important, but at the same time, you build tolerance and need more and more of that substance to generate the level of high you crave."

Once we're aware of scientific realities, we can begin to view our own situation from a more rational perspective. So, please, forgive yourself for what you didn't know. Forgive yourself for taking all the blame and being lied to by the world about the harms of alcohol.

This is your chance to overcome and survive. And you couldn't get here without first walking there. Let today be day one of the new you.

COMBATTING REAL-TIME TRIGGERS

As we've established, alcohol consumption elicits a powerful dopamine release. That makes us feel good, alleviating feelings of stress, anxiety, and pain. Of course, as soon as it starts wearing off, all those feelings come flooding back—the alcohol doesn't address the root of the problem. But your brain doesn't know that. It just wants another drink. Pretty soon, if you repeat the pattern enough times—using alcohol to numb or distract from uncomfortable feelings—your brain is conditioned to seek alcohol any time those feelings arise. It's a trigger.

Drinking triggers work similarly to Ivan Pavlov's famous experiment with dogs. In his experiment, dogs learned to associate a bell ringing with being fed. Once they'd made this association, they'd salivate just at the sound of the bell, whether food was present or not. Similarly, when we drink, our brains naturally begin to associate certain sources—like a time of day, a social situation, or even the feeling of stress—with the relief that alcohol provides. Over time, like the salivating dogs, your brain begins to expect alcohol in these moments. That makes it harder to resist the urge. You've accidentally primed yourself.

Triggers make sobriety feel unattainable. When that switch flips on, the rational brain turns off, and it's like we go on autopilot. Some people describe it as compulsion or cognitive dissonance. The feeling can be visceral: watering mouth, sweaty palms, racing heart, and a single-minded focus on getting alcohol in your vicinity. The body physically reacts to the mental pull, urging you toward the familiar comfort of alcohol.

I used to feel utterly powerless against my triggers. Once something signaled to my brain that I "needed" alcohol, obedience to the command seemed inevitable. There was no point in resisting—in my mind, it was over before it began.

When triggered, our brains don't distinguish between healthy and unhealthy solutions. They don't rationally assess the situation. They just react to the invisible, all-consuming pain points by seeking one particular solution at any cost. Like a restless itch, triggers cause us to believe that alcohol is the only escape from our discomfort. Yet we've learned this lie over years of habit as a defense mechanism against discomfort of all varieties. It's subtle, but we've fed the monster quietly each time we've given in to the craving.

Triggers may include things like:

- The five o'clock hour, universally known as the time it's appropriate to drink

- An argument with a spouse or friend
- Feeling disrespected, shut out, or hurt by a friend or family member
- Boredom
- Holidays, professional events, parties, concerts
- Negative emotions like depression, anxiety, grief, or loneliness
- Bad memories
- Stress of any kind
- Feeling sick
- Being somewhere where you always drink, like an airport
- Being around certain people
- Eating certain foods you associate with alcohol
- A mealtime at home or a dinner out

There's a technical term for this vicious cycle: hyperkatifeia. That's a long word for the negative emotional state we experience in the cycle of alcohol addiction. If we drink regularly to combat hardship or stress, negative emotions emerge more powerfully when we deprive ourselves of the "solution" we rely on. It's a cycle: we pass from intoxication to the negative experience of withdrawal, and then we anticipate the help of further intoxication and try to take hold of it.

ANTICIPATE YOUR TRIGGERS

Alcohol as medicine. Alcohol as relief. Alcohol as friend. Alcohol as reward. Alcohol as consolation. It's so versatile; it's there for any occasion, but it's always gone in the morning.

Triggers don't feel like mere bad habits—when we're triggered, we imagine we have a genuine need to drink. The challenge lies in distinguishing between the two and uncovering the deeper human need driving it all. The good news is that we can anticipate when we'll be triggered to use alcohol in these unhealthy ways.

Triggers are predictable. It's familiar to drink when the clock strikes five, or when an argument comes up with your spouse, or a holiday comes around. When we recognize our common triggers, we can begin to strategically tackle them. When do you find yourself most triggered? The "witching hour" when your child's naughty spirits are most activated? Perhaps the dreaded task of making dinner, or the dull end to your workday? Or perhaps it's more serious. You're grieving a profound loss. You're anxious about a relationship, job, or money. Sometimes, the pain from buried trauma or current life circumstances is so overwhelming we'd do anything to escape it. Immediately. Nothing else matters.

Our triggers are carved over time, and they develop out of desperation. Like a single drop of water falling onto a rock, the first drink to ease stress may have seemed insignificant. But when one drop turns into many, the water eats a hole into the stone, leaving a lasting impact.

Alcohol affects each of us differently. We are biologically and chemically wired differently, with varying genetics, sensitivities, temptations, coping mechanisms, and affinities. The social and emotional patterns we inhabit are diverse and complex. In other words, comparison is never wise. But whatever sparks our drinking desires to life, we can prepare for the moment with tangible strategies, resources and a plan of action. In the appendix of this book, I've shared a full list of tools and strategies to use in these moments.

RECLAIM YOUR POWER IN CHRIST

When a trigger arrives, we may feel powerless to combat the urges—but we *aren't*. Zoom in on truth: We don't *have* to drink. If someone locked me in a cage without access to alcohol, I wouldn't be able to take a drink, and eventually, that desire to do so would pass. I'd survive that moment. I know that's a drastic example, but it's necessary to illustrate what's possible when it feels impossible. We convince our minds and bodies of what's possible simply by *doing* it. It's always hardest the first time.

Jesus tells us, "Truly, I say to you, if you have faith like a grain of mustard seed, you will say to this mountain, 'Move from here to there,' and it will move, and nothing will be impossible for you" (Matthew 17:20). You've probably heard that verse before, but don't let repetition rob you of its truth. Do you *really* believe in God's promises? Now is the time to put that faith to work. We cannot trust our feelings to carry us out of this, because they will convince us we can't do it.

Think of what happens when a mom drops a child off at school or a playdate. So often, that kid wails, "Mama!" As a mom, I can tell you that it's *so* hard to resist going back over, scooping my kid up, and catering to their separation anxiety. But the healthy thing is for a child to learn independence, to trust that their mom *will* come back. Our feelings during triggered moments are similar. They tug so powerfully that turning away from the longing to drink feels like tearing yourself away from a beloved child.

What usually happens when Mom comes back to pick up her child? Usually, I find my daughter playing happily with other kids. The teachers tell me that her crying subsides after I leave. Everything turns out to be okay. The feeling triggered by my departure dissipates once she realizes she would survive if I weren't there. To be clear, I don't want to blame my child or fault her for missing me. But as a mom, I need to break the mental association so that she could learn that when I step away, she will survive—and even have fun. It's hard, but I'm glad that I can be strong enough to give her that gift of freedom and confidence.

We have to do the same for ourselves. We need to step out of that one-dimensional perspective and step into faith. *Millions* of people have overcome alcohol dependence. This isn't impossible. We can hear testimony after testimony of deliverance, holding them up as proof that even in the most hopeless circumstances, God makes a way.

Of course, unbelievers experience sobriety too, and don't credit God with helping them do it. But I think we can still look at their stories as testimonies of God's goodness. In the words of one of my favorite worship songs, "Waymaker," "Even when we don't see it, you're working." I think that God pursues the lost through many avenues, and does so until their last breath. They may not credit his help for their recovery, but he was there whether they knew it or not.

Having a strong faith doesn't mean you always feel fully confident about recovery, or that you don't worry about outcomes. But it does mean that you believe in something you can't see yet. It means you put your life in God's hands, despite your fears, doubts, and confusion. It means you believe you will survive, even though it feels like you won't.

Once you take all the pressure off yourself, you can healthily take up a mantle of responsibility—which is graciously lightened by our Lord: "'My grace is sufficient for you, for my power is made perfect in weakness.' Therefore I will boast all the more gladly of my weaknesses, so that the power of Christ may rest upon me" (2 Corinthians 12:9). Thank God he didn't make us dependent solely on our own strength. Today's world tells women to save themselves, love themselves, and find themselves. That's the wrong answer. We have a role to play, but we are not the remedy. He's the solution.

In a sermon, the pastor Alistair Begg once said, "Don't ask me how I *feel*. Ask what I *know* about God." I want to tattoo that on my forehead. Our feelings are fleeting and unreliable. But what's true about God? God's truth is immovable, unchangeable, covenanted. Don't just say you believe it. Actually believe it.

Our triggers have power only when we deliver their demands. They'll soon shut down when they realize we refuse to do so anymore. We know that God is sovereign and that only he holds the swirling of the universe in his hands. By the power of the Holy Spirit, God has given you the ability to say "no." And He's promised to help you do it.

MANAGING THE PAIN IN BETTER WAYS

Pain is inevitable, but we have control over how we cope with it. You've been using unhealthy tools to cope with uncomfortable parts of life, but now you know there are alternatives for that. Let's consider some of the healthy tools we have available.

When we think of "spiritual" tools, we might think of prayer, Scripture, and worship. We can rely on these, but God has provided us even more to help us overcome—friendships, family relationships, mentors, marriages, church family, Biblically grounded books, podcasts, support groups. And we have healthy coping mechanisms like breath work, exercise, laughter, and music. We can put God first in our journey and also deploy the many modes of recovery that prove helpful.

In the *American Journal of Preventive Medicine*, researchers Mary Njeri Wanjau and Holger Möller find that physical activity helps significantly reduce anxiety. Physical fitness and other hobbies can be rich ways to fill the space that drinking once took up in their lives. For this reason, organizations like The Phoenix, a free, sober fitness group that uses exercise and human connection, have emerged. What a powerful combination that is. Instead of retreating to the isolation of our tormented minds, we can reach out to someone and do something together. I'd recommend creating a list of people you can call or text when the desire hits.

Beyond that, developing a plan of action steps to work through in hard moments can be helpful. That list might include things like:

- Spend five minutes outside
- Take ten deep breaths
- Say one short prayer
- Call or text one safe person
- Read three Bible verses
- Chug a glass of water
- Open a nonalcoholic beverage

- Eat a snack
- Listen to a worship song
- Sit in silence for two minutes
- Leave the house
- Take a short walk or jog

Some of these steps may seem convoluted and full of unnecessary detours. But if it gets us to our destination, that extra time and effort is worth it.

We can remember and rationally remind ourselves that walking *through* a challenge is healthier and more productive than drowning in it with alcohol. Drinking the problem doesn't kill it. It just waits at the bottom, ready for your glass to empty again.

Now that we know our triggers and why they're popping up, we are empowered to take imperfect steps forward, with a lot of grace built in. With God's help, you can eventually disempower the triggers and traumas that have been controlling you. Start small, but know that most everyone who is sober was once where you are today. They felt it was impossible. But everything feels impossible until it's done.

As they say in AA, it works if you work it. "Working it" means honestly applying new lessons. You ask yourself why you want a drink, and find an answer before you get one. You take the steps, silly as they may seem, to avoid drinking when you don't want to. You stay connected to those who can support you in your ultimate goal of cutting back or quitting.

While you're working it, you will mess it up. Screw-ups, relapse, and trying again are baked into this process. Most people have a relapse story. And even if you never drink again, you will repeat some other unhealthy behavior or action. Self-compassion, the practice of treating yourself with the same kindness, understanding, and patience that you would offer someone else, is an ongoing need here.

When we "work it"—the tools and healthy ideas we're learning now—we are free to make better choices in the future. Forgive yourself for choices you made long ago without fully understanding their consequences. In hindsight, you might have chosen differently.

PAUSE & REFLECT

- What have you discovered by digging into this subject?
- How is alcohol unhelpful or detracting from your larger purpose as a Christian, woman, or mother?
- What would it look and feel like to glance back at your younger self and have compassion for her?
- How would you explain the difference between guilt and shame in your own words?
- What's one thing you might say to a friend if she were in your position?
- How can you be kind to yourself today in light of what you've learned?

SEVEN

THE HEART OF THE MATTER

IT TAKES REAL INTENTION TO set aside time and mental space for this process of personal discovery. Once the mind opens to a conversation about your history of drinking, unexpected insights begin to emerge. It may be a memory, a realization, or a word from the Lord. With heightened awareness, you will recognize the historical footprints that alcohol has left in your life.

The goal here isn't just to graze the surface; we want to get down to the root, which takes time. Think about how many years it took to get here.

If you haven't begun, it's time for a deep audit into your relationship with alcohol. At the end of this chapter, I've provided a comprehensive survey for you to use. Honestly, lots of us would rather run six miles than dissect our childhood in therapy for an hour. But lasting transformation—the way we get to *wanting to want* to quit drinking—requires us to go deep. Uncomfortably deep.

It wasn't fun for me. I had a somewhat idyllic childhood. Who was I to complain when I had so much? Fears of appearing ungrateful stopped me from assessing what led me to dysfunctional drinking. But as I considered, I realized that my parents expressed love through action rather than words. I remember being told I was "too emotional." I internalized an idea that feelings were inconvenient details to push through. My parents had both had far more hardship growing up than I did, and at that time, society had few outlets for them. Instead, they learned resilience through action. They passed their experiences on to me, even when my heart ached for understanding.

Resilience is important, but so are healthy coping mechanisms, like a supportive community and reliable habits, that create a protective buffer between you and alcohol when cravings or triggers arise.

I learned in therapy that I avoided criticizing my parents because it felt like a betrayal of my love for them. I didn't want to admit that their imperfections could have influenced me negatively. Of course, as a parent now, I see things more clearly. We *all* have lingering childhood issues—generational minefields perpetuated by those who came before. Ignoring them only buries them deeper, turning them into pressure-cooked problems that scorch our hearts and poison our souls. And yes, our children will one day have to process the things we passed along to them. But you know what? The healthier we can get now, the easier that task will be for our kids.

Buried pain and unresolved issues are usually part of the internal turmoil that drives us to numbness when other things get hard. That's what I had to get to, and get through.

Imagine a future free from the hold of alcohol. That version of you isn't someone else. It could be *you*. Keep moving forward, and refuse to give up.

One first step is getting quiet enough to hear the little girl inside of you. What did your younger self need that she didn't get? What does she need now? I know this kind of exercise can feel odd or maybe even silly, but there's a reason it's been so transformative to many people. "Three things are striking about inner child work," writes John Bradshaw in *Coming Home: Reclaiming and Healing Your Inner Child*. "The speed with which people change when they do this work; the depth of that change; and the power and creativity that result when wounds from the past are healed."

Inner child work can sound "woo woo" to some (it did to me!), but parts of it are worth exploring even if you don't adopt the whole concept.

Children naturally develop coping mechanisms to survive: people pleasing, dissociation, numbing out through TV or food or video games. These habits can and often do shift into adult versions of themselves as time goes by. For example, up to 35 percent of those dependent on alcohol or other drugs have also had eating disorders, according to the blog post "The Link Between Eating Disorders and Substance Use" from the National Alliance for Eating Disorders. That's a rate eleven times greater than the general population. Both of these challenges are part of my story. I've learned that if we don't deal with our issues, things only move in one direction. If we don't deal with the root issue, we're destined to continue punting it down the road with unhealthy behaviors.

When we are children, we are profoundly shaped by the adults in our lives. We learn from them to respond and behave in certain ways. Those coping mechanisms from childhood feel *just* as essential as the drink feels to the drinker. That's where we must go now.

Here was the kicker for me: It took me until I was well into adulthood to understand that my parents could be wrong—or imperfect. Sounds insane now, but that's how much I revered them. At some point, I stood up straight and lovingly told my mom that I liked my emotional, heart-on-my-sleeve self, and I didn't think there was anything wrong with that. In recognizing and establishing this about myself, I was standing up for the little girl who always felt her emotions were a weakness. Healing your inner child is just unlearning the negative behaviors we picked up as kids. It doesn't have to mean anything more than that.

In this focused mode, you'll uncover insights and connections about why you drink. Prepare for an "aha" moment that makes sense of your choices, habits, and years of struggle. So, let's go back there. Return to the beginning, before you knew you were drinking to survive. Why do you think you drank in the early days or years? Why do you think you keep doing it? It probably started before you were aware of it and before alcohol began distorting your pain. It intertwined with your very being, saturating brain signals and disrupting natural healing processes. You unknowingly dug chemical holes and serotonin-laced shortcuts to relief in the recesses of your mind every time you took a drink. By the time you realized the problem, alcohol had already made its impression on your mind.

BEFORE WE KNEW

So many women have succumbed to the wiles of alcohol without realizing where it would lead them. For some, it started in high school or college. For others, the subtle tipping point into dysfunctional drinking came later.

Consider some of the experiences of women I've met in recovery groups: Laura drank socially without an issue until she hit her late thirties, when marriage problems and job stress took their toll. Renee had no issues with alcohol until her children left home and an empty nest left her feeling purposeless and sad. Jamilah, a mother of seven, who didn't begin problem drinking until her youngest was five.

Like these women, for many of us, things can shift from casual drinking to alcohol dependence in a blink: The first time you turn to drinking alone to rid yourself of a feeling. The moment you find yourself unsatisfied with a glass or two, but can't pinpoint why. The realization that specific tasks are more manageable with the hum of alcohol in your system, nudging you to drink every time those tasks arise.

It is decidedly uncomfortable to be where you are right now. Five years in, I *still* have work to do, and always will. That refinement and sanctification is present for all of us until the end—and it's a beautiful privilege to do this work alive and well in the world. There's a saying that we start by doing what's necessary, then do what's possible. And then suddenly, we're doing the impossible.

Don't start with the impossible thing. Start with the small, necessary thing.

Psychiatrist David Burns wrote about a simple equation in his book *Feeling Good*: Resistance = Pain x Suffering.

When you resist the pain, or what actor Matthew Perry called "the big, terrible thing" in his memoir about addiction, it doesn't eliminate pain but compounds it. Could you be avoiding a painful memory or unresolved trauma? Are you resisting the inner call to face it now and break free from using alcohol as a form of self-medication? This unremedied pain is the "resistance" we discussed earlier. What's more, it can be manipulated by the Evil One, who is working to stifle your coming transformation. The resistance is so dang strong here that you know this transformation is a big one.

Eliminating alcohol is not a cure-all. In fact, sobriety tends to reveal to you that drinking has been your convenient scapegoat. I blamed alcohol for everything, believing it was my biggest problem. Conveniently, quitting would magically fix everything else—or so I thought. But the truth isn't that cut and dried. Giving up alcohol absolutely improved my life, but I had much to work through. I'd masked my insecurities and fears with the toxic filter of alcohol for so long. Thankfully, there's no timetable here. This is lifetime work, and you can tackle each part one at a time.

Once you see the past through this new lens, the colors change forever. You can't neatly fold those memories back up and tuck them away. Some have been buried for decades—perhaps even forgotten. Now is the time to unfold, sort through, and let go of what no longer serves you.

THE STRUGGLE IS REAL

Did you know that, according to a policy briefing published by the UK's Mental Health Foundation, rates of self-harm in women have tripled in recent years—and that misusing alcohol is considered a method of self-harm? There are also unprecedented rates of alcoholism in mothers of young children. In the *Journal of Addiction Medicine*, researchers from RTI International found that moms of young children increased their drinking by 323 percent during the pandemic.

When we assess the rise, reason, and remedy for these numbers, it's easy to see how skyrocketing addiction is killing more women than ever. But knowing something factually doesn't always do the trick. We know this is happening—and happening to us—but how do we deal with it realistically? We're complex beings. We need more than data points to generate heart and behavior change.

Knowing *why* we want to quit drinking or cut back is incredibly helpful. When we look at quitting as a requirement or a punishment for bad behavior, we tend to lack internal motivation. Doing something from obligation feels entirely different from doing it from genuine desire. When I was in this position, I wondered: How could I possibly *want* to give up alcohol? I *wanted* to want to, but I didn't—yet.

GO DEEP WITH IT

Ask yourself why you want to quit drinking, or improve this part of your life. What core memories or significant thoughts rise?

Here's an example of what I wrote down in response to this question:

- Obedience to God
- My kids, because I don't want them to inherit this
- My marriage, because drinking caused fights and led to disruption
- My body, because alcohol is a cancerous toxin
- My peace, because I think about drinking all the time
- My focus, because I feel compelled to drink
- My sleep, and not waking up with regrets
- No more morning headaches or dehydration

- My whole body, mind and spirit, that they'd no longer be dictated to by a substance
- My reputation and character, that I wouldn't say or do anything foolish again because of alcohol

When we identify the reasons, we can find the compassion we need to love the person who made the choices to drink.

Here's a way to experiment with this: Consider what it would sound and feel like to share a part of your story out loud. Try it out all by yourself to get started. Speaking even one sentence of concern into the world can be really powerful.

If you're not quite ready to share with your voice, starting with words on paper is an effective start. Try out free writing: writing without any hesitation or time for editing, adjustment of ideas, or fixing mistakes. It's a purposefully messy and unstructured process that allows the brain to empty everything out. Such writing can be an intensely healing exercise, and it's been crucial for folks recovering from conditions like PTSD.

On his podcast, Dr. Andrew Huberman has spoken about how revisiting trauma through writing can be distressing. But when you move through the distress, engaging in a structured narrative exercise like this increases activity in vital areas of the brain related to reducing symptoms and processing past traumas. It sounds simple, but something about writing unlocks a part of the brain that thinking, speaking, or reading alone does not. In a study published in *Complementary Therapies in Clinical Practice*, researchers Oliver Glass and Mark Dreusicke found that a six-week daily personal writing practice boosted resilience while reducing depression and perceived stress. By the end, 35 percent of participants with depression no longer experienced symptoms.

Note that writing or speaking about these topics often draws out intense emotions. I would ask that you allow these feelings to surface, because they can lead to important breakthroughs.

YOUR EMOTIONS MATTER

I think we should love ourselves, but we need to be honest: There will never be enough "self-love" to cover all our problems. This concept is important to consider because it's so ingrained in female, secular culture. Sadly, it's often twisted to offer promises it simply can't fulfill. It can also be overspiritualized, leading us to put ourselves in the place of God. That may sound drastic, but for those without faith, it's sometimes the reality. Unfortunately, if self-love is the only source of love we rely on, it goes toxic. Why? Because we are sinners *in need* of a Savior, not a people who can save themselves. On the other hand, we are *also* beloved children of God, whom he views with the highest value. That's the paradox of the gospel.

Some Christian cultures denigrate the notion of self-love entirely. Paul writes, "In the last days . . . people will be lovers of self, lovers of money, proud, arrogant, abusive . . . swollen with conceit, lovers of pleasure rather than God" (2 Timothy 3:1-4). This passage could be interpreted to say that self-love is on par with abuse, pride, and arrogance. But, that last part, which reads "rather than lovers of God," is key. Loving ourselves isn't the problem. The problem is when we love ourselves more *than* we love God. The law of Moses directs us to "love your neighbor as yourself" (Leviticus 19:18). And Paul writes that "no one ever hated his own flesh, but nourishes and cherishes it, just as Christ does the church" (Ephesians 5:29).

Because Scripture never tells us directly to love ourselves, we can assume it's the default position. God created us with the capacity and natural ability to love ourselves. He doesn't want us to hate ourselves.

Although we were created with the divine capacity to love rightly, the fall distorted that gift. Yet, through the redemptive work of Christ, we are being sanctified and restored to love rightly.

God knew we would sin, but he created us anyway, forming a way to stay with him despite our imperfections. Yet our view of self-love as Christians differs from that of the world.

In a secular framework, self-love is often seen as the solution to brokenness. But in Christian theology, self-love results from being healed and made whole through Christ. It's not the means to an end. Rather, it's the fruit of living confidently in who we are in Christ.

For the believer, self-love is not the remedy—it's the result. It's not the means to wholeness but the fruit of knowing who we are in Christ. When we embrace our identity in him, we begin to see ourselves with the same grace he already offers.

Romans 3:23-24 spells it out: "For all have sinned and fall short of the glory of God, and are justified by his grace as a gift." God made a way for us. We are his creations, crafted with the incredible capacity to love, because we were made in his image. We can take our sins seriously without ignoring our God-given sensitivities and the valuable emotions he created. Our feelings, along with our consciousness, are part of our image-bearing nature. God made us this way on purpose! We shouldn't be slaves to our feelings, nor should we ignore or deny them altogether. Instead, we need to give them the balanced value they deserve in the context of our entire being.

What does it look like to love oneself as a Christian? It means having a healthy understanding of our position as servants of the King *and* his beloved creations. In other words, it means knowing our place *and* recognizing our value. What if Paul hadn't accepted God's forgiveness? Peter? Moses? Mary Magdalene? A long line of fallen believers that God used for great things came before us. Murderers, adulterers, liars, and, yes, even alcoholics.

Did their failures stop God's plan to change lives, fulfill prophecies, or write his story? No. In fact, I love that the Bible is full of failures. If one of us were writing the book for our religion, they probably wouldn't include the miserable failures of their greatest leaders. But God did. "God relentlessly offers his grace to people who do not deserve it, or seek it, or even appreciate it after they have been saved by it," writes Tim Keller in his book *Generous Justice*.

We can rest assured that we're not worse than anyone else. God showed us through his chosen people that he offers endless grace upon grace. There is forgiveness everlasting.

THE SIN OF IT ALL

Where's the line for sin when it comes to alcohol? Unlike, say, adultery or theft, drinking alcohol isn't a sin on its own (at least at face value). And as we've discussed, alcohol dependence or addiction is not just behavioral—it's also emotional and chemical. The urge to use it as a coping mechanism has been shaped by each individual's history, environment, and genetics. So while all human downfalls are ultimately rooted in sin, don't exclusively define your struggle through sin. The Genesis account of the fall reveals that the sins of Adam and Eve brought suffering and death into the world, leading to much of what you and I are feeling today.

Let's explore this a bit more. Paul confirms in Romans 5:12 that "sin came into the world through one man, and death through sin." And we all sin; we're all part of the problem (Romans 3:23). Sin always produces suffering, questioning, and struggle, opening the door to the forces of evil in the world (2 Corinthians 4:4) And because of Adam's sin, there is disorder and brokenness even when it doesn't make sense (Romans 8:20). It's in this context that you can think about your relationship with alcohol, even if it's more like a nagging sense that your drinking doesn't honor God.

When Eve took the fruit from the serpent in the Garden, it didn't seem like a big deal, right? It's an apple, for goodness' sake. But it wasn't about the apple. It was about the obedience.

In the same way, it's not about the wine. It's not about having permission to enjoy things. It's about what God's saying to you as an individual, just as he spoke to Eve. We can't change the past, but the future is a blank slate. Let's listen to the counsel of Hebrews 12:1, which tells us to "throw off everything that hinders and the sin that so easily entangles. And let us run with perseverance the race marked out for us" (NIV).

Is alcohol "easily entangling" you in a way that thwarts the "race marked out" for you? Don't ask, "Is alcohol a sin?" Ask if it's hindering you from pursuing God's path for you.

Instead of asking, "Can I do this?" Ask, "Am I free?"

"You cannot be set free, Jesus says in Luke 4:18, until you recognize that you're a captive," says pastor Tim Badal in a 2019 sermon at the Village Bible Church. "What is it that you're habitually obsessing over that keeps you from a right relationship with God? Name it. Declare it. Then stop making excuses for it." I want to get clear on one thing: The medical reality of a physical addiction isn't sinful. However, some of the behavior choices we make within the workings of the addiction can be.

Regardless of what drives sinful choices—be it nurture, nature, chemistry, genetics, physiology—sinful behavior is still sinful. For example, a person may have had a traumatic childhood, but it would still be wrong to enact similar traumas on their own child, even if they suffer from PTSD.

Addiction is ultimately a search *for* God, but we're looking in the wrong places. That's why addictive behaviors can be confusing: we're seeking something good, not bad. That said, there are still consequences and realities to address. "Even if addiction is a misguided search for God, the actions flowing from that search—when they harm ourselves or others and contradict the known will of God, can still be sinful," says Wesleyan pastor Scott Rhyno. The good news is that it is exactly the kind of sin Jesus came to save us from, the kind of sin the Holy Spirit empowers us to overcome.

While many people can hide their search for God in a less obvious vice, the alcoholic reflects pain more sensationally. We aren't more screwed up than the next person. Our modes of expression are just louder and more destructive. No matter what the struggle, however, no situation is too difficult for God.

WHAT GOD SAYS IS TRUE

At one point in my life, I wondered how I'd ever stop bingeing and starving. And I thought my struggles were a reflection of my spiritual state. I thought I'd failed as a Christian to be where I was.

But that feeling just made me want to hide and binge more, compounding the shame I already felt. Only when I detached my problem from my perceived strength of faith could I walk forward in the clarity of being known and loved by God.

Here's a significant realization I've come to: Problems with alcohol aren't some special kind of bad. I wasn't unique because I used alcohol to cope. Alcoholism felt monumental to talk about. But, once I talked about it, I realized I was just one of many moms trying to get through the day. Dealing with unhealthy coping mechanisms is something all of us have to do, not just alcoholics. And because we don't have to be "good" to earn a spot in God's kingdom, we can choose to do good out of authentic love. No need for guilt, shame, or fear.

The fact that we can choose a better pathway, knowing that our belovedness is safe either way, shifts the paradigm significantly. Living such spiritual autonomy naturally produces flourishing. We don't have to do good. We want to.

I'm asking you to believe what God says about you is true: You are loved and valuable despite your sin and struggle. You were born a sinner, but you will die a saint. You are the prodigal child returning, and God doesn't recall why you left. Please accept that as a Christian, you are always acceptable. God can swap a mindset of despair and disappointment for hope and redemption.

PAUSE & ASSESS

The following exercise is to develop self-compassion and understanding. It's not meant to make you stop drinking today, forever. Just think of it as a chance for the powerful work of observation and intentional processing.

If you've never assessed your drinking past in this way, it may unlock some unexpected insights. Don't have any expectations as you run through the questions. Just be as open, honest, and detailed as you can with your answers.

Take some time to answer these questions. Look over your answers and identify patterns, revelations, and concepts God may reveal through this exercise.

If you can, find a photo of yourself as a little girl. With that photo nearby and a journal or blank document opened on your screen, answer the following questions:

- ☐ What would you say to her before life was corrupted by hardship, loss, failure, or other challenges?
- ☐ What do you want for her?
- ☐ How does she deserve compassion?
- ☐ What does she need to hear right now?

On another blank page, walk through the questions about your history with alcohol. Consider how having a deep awareness of your history could shift your perspective.

This will allow space for God to show up and work inside this fresh framework of thought. It'll help eliminate the noise pollution of your intrusive thoughts so that the Holy Spirit's whisper can break through.

Assessment Questions:

1. When did you start drinking?

2. Why did you start? (Just give your best guess.)

3. What messages did you hear about alcohol as a young person?

4. When did your drinking become problematic?

5. Where or when have you felt shame about drinking?

6. When have you felt shame about yourself more generally?

7. What do you think God thinks or feels about your drinking?

8. What are your triggers now?

9. What has your drinking cost you in the last one to three years?

10. What would life look like without alcohol?

Questions to Assess: "Do I Have a Problem?"

There are few ways to assess your history with drinking. The simplest assessment I've seen is called the CAGE method. CAGE stands for Cut Down, Annoyed, Guilty, and Eye-Opener. It consists of the following four questions:

☐ Have you ever felt you should cut down on your drinking?

☐ Have people annoyed you by criticizing your drinking?

☐ Have you ever felt bad or guilty about your drinking?

☐ Have you ever had a drink first thing in the morning to steady your nerves or get rid of a hangover?

And here are some questions from the Objective Structured Clinical Examination (OSCE) on alcohol use:

☐ How often do you drink?

☐ How much do you drink when you do?

☐ Is there anything that makes you drink more or less in a day?

☐ Where do you drink?

☐ Who do you drink with?

☐ When did you first notice an increase in the amount of alcohol you were drinking?

- ☐ Was there anything going on at the time that played a role in this?
- ☐ Have you ever tried to stop drinking before?
- ☐ What happened when you tried?
- ☐ Did you have any support?
- ☐ Why do you think it was unsuccessful?
- ☐ Do you feel a compulsion or need to drink?
- ☐ How important is drinking to you?
- ☐ If you stop drinking, do you notice that you feel down, angry, or anxious?
- ☐ Has alcohol impacted any of your personal relationships? How has it affected them?
- ☐ When did you first notice a shift in your alcohol consumption?
- ☐ When did it go from something you rarely thought about to a bad habit that caused wince and worry?

EIGHT

THE BAD THEOLOGY
OF CONTROL

IT'S TIME TO DITCH the "weak person" narrative many of us rely on. It's part of the bad theology of control—a mindset in which we erroneously think it's all on us.

In this mindset, we assume our struggle with alcohol is because we lack willpower or moral fortitude. But addiction and dependence don't work that way. Alcohol is engineered to alter the brain's pathways, making it extremely difficult, if not impossible, to break free from dependence through willpower alone.

Unfortunately, this thought process subtly undermines the core Christian understanding of grace, surrender, and the recognition of our human limitations. Abiding by such misguided thinking means we get all the blame and all the glory, but that is not the way of Christ. God's power is not contingent on our own strength. Rather, his power is made perfect in our weakness (2 Corinthians 12:9).

For Christian women struggling with alcohol, this false belief can be particularly damaging. It can lead to:

- *Shame and Isolation:* Women may feel immense shame for not being able to "control" their drinking, leading to isolation and preventing them from seeking help.

- *Spiritual Disconnect:* The belief that they are failing God can create a sense of spiritual disconnect, hindering their ability to experience God's grace and healing.
- *Relapse and Despair:* When efforts to control drinking fail, it can lead to relapse and a feeling of hopelessness, reinforcing the idea that they are inherently flawed or weak.

I was twenty when I first believed I had utterly failed as a Christian. I saw the depression and eating disorder that ruled my life as a lack of faith, a sad testament to the Christianity that I claimed was so important and life-changing. That's why it took me six years to make an appointment with a therapist. Just scheduling it felt sacrilegious. It was admitting defeat. It meant my faith just wasn't strong enough to overcome.

I felt like a ghost (and hoped I was to passersby) walking to my first appointment. Inside the small room of the therapist's office, I tapped my foot incessantly while waiting for the therapist to arrive. I'd taken the elevator up to the sixth floor of our local hospital and been buzzed through a door reading "Psychiatric" to get to my appointment. I was about to see our town's premier psychologist specializing in eating disorders, and I was on the floor with the most contentious population in the facility.

I'd spent the last six years in a brutal cycle of starving, bingeing, purging, overexercising, and despairing I'd ever return to the body peace and normalcy I knew as a child.

Before puberty hit, life was carefree, and I didn't think about the calories in lunchmeat or if I could make it to dinner on an eight-ounce container of organic yogurt. Back then, I didn't scheme about fitting in a five-mile run to work off the half of a blueberry bagel I ate for breakfast. I didn't spend weekends depressed in a darkened dorm room, downing a whole bag of Dunkin' Donuts and chocolate milk from the university cafeteria. In wild moments of triggered bingeing, I would eat until sickness came, barely able to walk down the hall as my body responded in shock and rejection to thousands of sugary calories.

By this time in my life, I was heavier than I'd ever been yet still starving myself half the time, which often led to bingeing and purging through laxatives and exercise. I'd heard about the fun and freedom of the first year of college, but my time wasn't measuring up, and I didn't know why. I existed in a thick fog of depression and obsession, punctuated by classes I nearly failed and occasional parties in which I drank to oblivion. It was in this desperation and depression that I finally considered therapy as a possible answer.

I wasn't opposed to therapy, but had grown up believing Christians really just needed more Jesus—not psychologists. So, in a way, when I made that first appointment, it felt a bit like letting God down. I couldn't control my eating, drinking, or depression. Clearly, I thought, I was lacking the fruits of the Spirit. I couldn't hack it in the real world on my faith alone.

REJECTING THE STIGMA

A significant stigma lingers around mental health treatment in Christian spaces. Decades ago, it was common for spiritual leaders to guide believers struggling with mental illness away from medical intervention and toward a more "faithful" avenue of prayer and self-discipline. Today, most Christian leaders advocate for therapy and medication when needed—but what is considered to constitute medical necessity is an argument on its own.

It's not uncommon today for more conservative Christian leaders to think of depression and anxiety as spiritual problems, even if they acknowledge more severe disorders as medical. In a 2024 panel at Grace Church of the Valley, pastor John MacArthur said, "There is no such thing as mental illness." He went on to say that conditions like PTSD, OCD, and ADHD are "myth[s]." His attitude isn't rare.

But if you or someone you love suffers from something like PTSD, you know it's not a myth. My husband's lifelong struggle with PTSD from his traumatic childhood isn't something he chose. It's taken years of therapy, hours of prayer, thousands of prescription pills, and brutal wrestling with God to reach the place of relative freedom in which he lives today.

Societal and faith-based understanding of mental illness has grown in recent decades, and most Christian leaders recognize it as a legitimate medical condition. In fact, in a interview for the *Desiring God* blog, the theologically conservative preacher John Piper said that if one can be helped by medicine, "in the short run especially, sometimes long term—then I think, in God's grace and mercy, we should take it as a gift from His hand."

The problem is that many people view this as an either-or situation. Either you turn to God, the true source of all joy, for healing, or you turn to modern psychiatric medicine and ignore any spiritual aspects of your struggle or your path to healing. The truth is that we need both. A study published in *Mental Health, Religion & Culture*, led by Jonathan Schettino and Natasha Olmos, found that people with a strong faith who take antidepressants and receive treatment are more likely to recover from temporary mental health problems in the long run. Those with an element of faith, especially in a faith community, have better odds on their road to recovery, because God created us to thrive in him and within his church. Similarly, researchers Judy Leung and Kin-Kit Li published in the journal *Healthcare* that religiously engaged individuals tend to experience fewer symptoms of depression and recover more quickly.

Led by the Great Physician, a triune path of healing—body, mind, and spirit—can unveil God's most wondrous miracles. That might look like:

- **Body**: Medical interventions (e.g., medication, health care)
- **Mind**: Psychological interventions (e.g., therapy, emotional processing)
- **Spirit**: Spiritual interventions (e.g., prayer, grace, Scripture, spiritual disciplines)

A holistic pathway that includes all the tools at our disposal is the best bet for healing.

I had no idea I'd been living under a web of lies about addiction. My psychologist recommended a round of antidepressants to get my brain to a more stable place. I reflexively rejected this suggestion, my young Christian mind immediately calling familiar memory verses to the surface: "The joy of the LORD is your strength" (Nehemiah 8:10) and "Do not be anxious in anything" (Philippians 4:6).

I believed that, as a Christian, I shouldn't "need chemicals" to be well. As someone who still owned T-shirts with phrases like "My lifeguard walks on water," my theology wasn't exactly refined. I don't know that anyone explicitly told me that antidepressants or therapy were wrong, but somehow I'd internalized the idea that faith was all I should need. My therapist seemed familiar with this response, responding kindly with a metaphor.

"If someone has cancer, we give them chemotherapy," she said. "Do you think that person shouldn't take that treatment just because they're a Christian?"

I hedged a bit, ultimately admitting that it wasn't wrong for someone with a physical ailment or disease to receive medical treatment to help them get better.

"Depression and eating disorder are just another kind of disease—in your mind—and antidepressants can be part of the remedy to that illness," she told me.

It was the first time I'd ever considered that my depression and my eating disorder might exist in a broader context than my own sinful choices, that maybe I hadn't put myself in this position, and that I deserved to receive care.

The ideas that pills could be God-ordained health care, and that my eating disorder might not be my fault, were pivotal.

This shift in the way I viewed mental health, which helped me realize I was deserving of care and help, would return years later when I replaced my eating disorder with alcohol use disorder. I didn't recognize the parallels then, even though the triggers felt similar. The moments of breakdown were often identical: time filled with my anxious thoughts, rejection or heartbreak of one kind or another, and a desire to numb out from the hardships and responsibilities of life.

As a Christian, can you relate to the spiritual layer of shame, secrecy, or just conviction when it comes to drinking? Consider this truth from Scripture: "There is therefore now no condemnation for those who are in Christ Jesus" (Romans 8:1). When we feel condemned, we can respond with truth. Accepting condemnation—the lie that we're not good enough and never will be—denies the saving grace Jesus has already given us. Yes, we are sinners—that's a sure thing. But we are also beloved children of God, struggling with a vice we never wanted to have. He tells us to "hide in the shadow of his wings" (Psalm 17:8) and that anywhere there is sin, his grace abounds "all the more" (Romans 5:20).

Those don't sound like the words of a harsh tyrant. That's because they are those of a loving, compassionate Father. Don't get me wrong—God certainly "executes judgment" (Psalm 75:7). But for the believer, Jesus' sacrifice on the cross covers all sins, all mistakes, all struggles—including drinking.

Can we treat ourselves with the same grace God offers? God says we have "received grace in place of grace already given" (John 1:16 NIV). We shouldn't choose to ignore God's grace and condemn ourselves. When we let go of the need to punish ourselves, we can move forward in the freedom of the desire to love and serve him.

What does that mean in reality? It means that even if you never got one ounce "better" from this struggle, God wouldn't love you any less, and your heavenly reward would not be in jeopardy. He loves you just as you are, even in your worst, most humiliating moments. And his grace covers all of it. Once we accept this premise, we can move forward in the context of true freedom.

In this freedom, we need not deny our whole, complex, emotional selves, no matter what some faith traditions are prone to suggest.

I'm so grateful to my therapist, who pulled back the curtain of my naive worldview to show me that Christians struggling with addiction, mental illness, or any other vice aren't just weak. If someone has cancer, they get chemo. If someone is diabetic, we give them insulin. If someone struggles with addiction, we get them the treatment they need—no matter how minor or overwhelming it may be.

DRINKING AND THE CHURCH

So many in the church silently struggle because of the stereotype that Christians shouldn't need help with an alcohol problem.

Teachers, doctors, business owners, pastor's wives, and stay-at-home moms—women across every profession, background, and belief system are grappling with the toxic pull of alcohol dependence, whether in subtle routines or full-blown addiction.

People don't see hidden alcoholism, so they don't address it. If no one's addressing it, it's easy to convince oneself there's no problem. If you have to convince yourself, something is up.

Because it's so hidden, we need to talk about it. Friends and family members don't even know to watch for drinking struggles. Show me a photo of six women in a Bible study, each of them looking happy and bubbly. I couldn't identify the alcoholic by her eyes or her clothes or her hair. We're simply hidden in plain sight, often desperate for someone to call us out and get it over with.

Unfortunately, women don't yet feel safe to share at church. I think there's a useful parallel with another difficult issue for women: unplanned pregnancy. In the blog post "Women Distrust Church on Abortion," Lifeway Research published findings that women name church as the last place they'd go for help in an unplanned pregnancy. Church should be a safe space, but it's often one where everyone knows you, your family, and your standing in the community. So it can feel like you could risk losing everything if people discover your secret. This is catastrophizing, but on the dark side of addiction or emergency, our minds aren't rational.

Addiction holds a similar stigma to an unplanned pregnancy because both are such stark representations of a certain kind of sin. Lust. Drunkenness. You're being exposed as "bad" when these circumstances come to light.

But this narrative that substance dependence is defined by sin and weakness must change. It's not that black and white—not even close. "Addiction doesn't just happen to people because they come across a particular chemical and begin taking it regularly," writes addiction researcher Maia Szalavitz in *Unbroken Brain*. "It is learned and has a history rooted in their individual, social, and cultural development." Christians and leaders in the church can learn more about the science of addiction to more accurately understand the experiences of women like me—and perhaps, like you. You should be able to walk forward knowing that your struggle is not just about a sin you committed years ago.

In an article titled "Strong-Willed But Not Successful," researcher Anke Snoek publishes findings that "strong willpower" doesn't equal much for recovery either. Rather, recovery is "dependent on developing strategies to preserve willpower by controlling the environment." It's more about how we position ourselves, the tools we use, and the higher truths we believe in than a physical act of will.

In other words, you can't recover all at once—it's a holistic process that takes time. Just as a risotto must be constantly stirred to reach perfection in cooking, our journey to freedom from alcohol requires diligence, maintenance, and commitment.

Knowing that and living it are different. It's especially tough for a girl baptized and bred in the evangelical church. (I still love my church upbringing, but as an adult, I know that its messaging can get misconstrued in childhood!) As a kid, I learned that if I was a good Christian, non-Christians would see Christ in me and "want what you have"—some inexplicable inner peace and joy. My entire life, I've wondered where that joy and peace were.

How could others want what I have, I thought, when I'm drunk and depressed? I thought that telling people what was happening in my life would ruin Jesus' reputation. It turns out that I gave myself *a lot* of credit for what only God could do. I thought God needed me to show people how great life was once you were saved, that your problems vanish and the joy of the Lord is always your strength. But that's not what the gospel is about.

You are not in control of anyone else's salvation, and nobody's salvation rests on you keeping your struggle a secret. Your brokenness in this area doesn't disqualify you from being an ambassador for Christ, right where you are. Though we remain imperfect, we are no longer slaves to sin (Romans 6:6-7). Rather, we are new creations, continually being renewed and made holy through the Spirit's work. That sanctification, through our salvation in Christ, ultimately sets us free from the power of sin in our lives. So while we are still capable of sin, we are no longer bound by it. Our spirits have been made alive in Christ, and the Spirit continually forms a life that reflects his love, holiness, and freedom.

That should not stop us from loving God well and telling others the good news: While we were still sinners, Christ died for us.

In that knowledge of our assured love and salvation, we can gladly admit our imperfection and take action, like speaking about our struggle. It's only through this process that we can heal from the pain that drew us to alcohol in the first place. Healing happens in the light of day, because shame is a vampire—it dies when the sun hits. Remember that Satan hides in dark corners, unable to operate in the presence of the Son.

The minute you step into the courage of a deep trust in your belovedness, the world becomes a sanctuary to heal.

And if you ever start to doubt your worth, return to Scripture:

> For I am convinced that neither death nor life, neither angels nor demons, neither the present nor the future, nor any powers, neither height nor depth, nor anything else in creation, will be able to separate us from the love of God that is in Christ Jesus our Lord. (Romans 8:38-39 NIV)

ADMITTING IT DOESN'T MEAN YOU'RE UNFIXABLE

If alcohol weren't a common problem, the millions of people in AA and Al-Anon wouldn't exist. Alcohol is a highly addictive substance, and it's been pushed on us for hundreds of years—a poison disguised as a remedy.

In the theology of control, we make the struggle with alcohol (or anything!) the entire book, rather than just one chapter or detail of our story. As women, as human beings, we are so much more than that. Yet, this theology tells us that our failures define worth.

Healing and change aren't about proving our strength. Rather, they're about recognizing an utter dependence on God and acknowledging our inherent value beyond our mistakes. In other words, you are not just a woman who drank too much, or a weak person that can't get it together. The only thing you need to do is keep getting back up and trying again.

Think about it like this: When someone has diabetes, managing that condition doesn't define them. Same thing with something like colitis or cancer. No one blames someone for having these medical conditions, but the affected individuals do have to care for themselves appropriately to ensure they don't get sick.

It's similar to accepting our condition as sinners. We did not choose our sinfulness; it is ingrained in our fallen bodies and faculties. By admitting our powerlessness, we can shift from self-help (which will always fail) to a rescue found only within the promises of God. Remember, that's the first step of AA: admitting you are powerless over alcohol.

To be clear, it's not just alcohol. Poet W.H. Auden once noted in *A Certain World* that "all sins tend to be addictive." We're all doomed without Christ. Everyone exists in the powerlessness that comes with not being God. Without the blood of Jesus, we are powerless over *everything*—sin, vice, habit, or doubt. Alcohol is one iteration of this, a particularly visceral instance of our need for greater hope and strength than we have as mere mortals.

I'm thankful, however, that "we do not have a high priest who is unable to sympathize with our weaknesses, but one who in every respect has been tempted as we are, yet without sin. Let us then with confidence draw near to the throne of grace, that we may receive mercy and find grace to help in time of need" (Hebrews 4:15-16).

God is the ultimate answer, but he graciously provides us with shepherds, supports, and comforts. One of the greatest tools he's given us is the chance to process, heal, and walk through our challenges with a loving community. This is the foundation of twelve-step programs and why they've proven so successful over the decades. And engaging in this communal work levels the playing field of life. Walking through the church lobby, we needn't hide the tears we cried for a diagnosis. We needn't grasp to maintain perfection. These internal struggles are real for all of us, whether we're stay-at-home moms, lawyers, teachers, or firefighters. To hide them is spiritually toxic and, as I hope you're beginning to see, unnecessary.

We are whole people, crafted intricately and purposefully, with God's signature appearing in every individual fingerprint that ever was or will be. We are more than our pain and weakness. When we let our struggle film over everything else, we give it far too much power.

Consider your roles in life—mother, worker, friend, sister. What do you do well? What gifts has God given you? We can acknowledge our human depravity while also believing God when he says we are made in his image and that it is very good (Genesis 1:27-31). I'm inspired by traditional Native American art, in which creators believe in designing work with deliberate imperfection to acknowledge that perfection belongs to God alone. I think that applies here too. Saint Augustine writes in *Confessions*, "God loves each of us as if there were only one of us."

Our weaknesses do not cancel out God's goodness, which is imprinted on our hearts. God loves, uses, and redeems all of us despite ourselves.

PAUSE & REFLECT

- What negative messages have you heard about mental health, antidepressants, therapy, or self-compassion as it relates to your faith?
- When have you fallen into believing the lies of the theology of control?
- How might those messages be influencing your view of your struggles or road to recovery?
- What's one positive way you've used self-compassion in the past?

NINE

INVITING GOD IN

IN THE MOVIE *Inside Out 2*, the emotion named Anxiety constantly fights to take control of the main character's mind. When Anxiety seizes complete mastery of the "mind control board," she pushes every other emotion aside, spiraling into such a frenzy that she loses control entirely.

Watching that scene reminded me of what happens when we try to deal with everything in our strength. We're not supposed to do that—and that's why it doesn't work. Instead of calling up Anxiety, we should ping Prayer to assist.

A consistent prayer habit serves as a constant reminder that God is our anchor, inviting us to release our tight grip on control and strength. I'm not saying it's easy, but I want you to find out what happens when you accept that invitation to let go. The more we surrender our pain to the Holy Spirit, the less toxic it becomes moving forward. Letting go isn't a one-time thing. Rather, it's a daily, intentional one. Sometimes you won't do it. Sometimes, you'll wish you had. But you always have another chance to try again tomorrow.

THE POWER AND PURPOSE OF PRAYER

One way to cultivate a habit of prayer, offering you a steady center to return to, is by learning simple, repeatable prayers to recite at specific times.

We didn't have many rituals in my family growing up, but one stands out for how routinely mom employed it: a nighttime prayer she recited over my sisters and me each night at bedtime: "Jesus, tender shepherd, hear me. Bless thy little lamb tonight. Through the darkness, be down near me, and keep me safe till morning light."

I could say it in my sleep. I started praying it over each of my children at birth. I'll never forget it.

If you grew up in a more evangelical space, liturgical prayers may not be as familiar to you, but there is a reason such prayers have stood the test of time. They embed themselves in your mind, and they will surface at the right time.

AA is famous for its members' repetition of a condensed version of the Serenity Prayer. Its words are so powerful: "God, grant me the serenity to accept the things I cannot change, courage to change the things I can, and wisdom to know the difference." It's brief yet filled with everything someone might need in a difficult moment. Of course, it's especially relevant for those struggling with substance abuse. The Serenity Prayer is just one of many available to repeat and store in your memory. Books like *Liturgies for Hope* or *Every Moment Holy* are good places to start looking for prayers that fit your situation.

You can also create your own. If you like to write and create, consider writing your own short prayers to read and remember. Simple Scripture verses are also more than enough. I've added a list of my favorites later in this chapter. God instructs the Israelites to bind his words "as a sign on your hand . . . between your eyes" and "write them on the doorposts of your house and on your gates" (Deuteronomy 6:8-9). These words are life. The more deeply ingrained they are on our hearts and in our minds, the more vividly they can animate and assist us consistently.

In a chaotic world filled with mixed messages, reaching back for solid, memorable truths to root us down appears to work. I think it's because of how effective and comforting their familiar words and calming cadences are to our overstimulated, weary souls. We could all use more tools of the Spirit, like prayers buried deep in the recesses of our minds and hearts, to pull out when those challenging moments surface. It's healing to have something we can immediately hang on to before slipping into chaos.

There's a reason for that. In an interview for the "Working Knowledge" blog, Harvard Business School professor Gerald Zaltman says that 95 percent of our decisions are subconscious. Meanwhile, Joel Hoomans cites research in a blog post for "The Leading Edge" that we make at least thirty-three thousand choices daily. We have more power over some of those under-the-radar choices than we think, but it takes a fresh mindset, new habits, and consistency to trigger a lasting and significant change.

Can we build rituals that ground us in our faith first? Can we construct a solid architecture for our inner lives shaped by the truth of what we know about God? Consider a habit that you have already reached for that naturally leads to him.

Joni Eareckson Tada became a quadriplegic at seventeen, and she told me she couldn't have gotten through the last sixteen years without rooting herself into daily habits of worship—going to God in the midst of her pain and praising him. Several years ago, I interviewed Joni after she published a children's book about the hope of heaven, which is a particularly significant idea for someone in her condition.

She spoke about the many nights she wakes up in severe, unrelenting pain. Such pain in the dark of night—whether physical or emotional—is nearly unbearable. Because she has no control over the situation, she often begins to sing hymns in bed, summoning the Holy Spirit to her side, knowing she can't battle this alone. In her book *Ordinary People, Extraordinary Faith*, she writes, "Deny your weakness, and you will never realize God's strength in you."

We may not be facing a life of physical paralysis, but when our spirits are harnessed by addiction, abuse, and lies from the devil that we can never be free, God's work in and through us will be stifled. We miss out when we neglect prayer. A consistent prayer and praise practice can change your mindset and decrease your desire to drink in the long term.

TURNING TO PRAYER

In his book *Prayer*, Tim Keller writes that "prayer turns theology into experience." Theology is what we believe about God. When we pray, we put that belief into action.

We pray to know God, and the more we know him, the easier it is to access him in moments of hardship. The more we know and understand his character, the more we are naturally drawn to be more like him, to strengthen our faith, and to believe that he is able to do what we need. Prayer is one fundamental way to know him more, hear him more clearly, and hold onto him more fervently. This is an organic process that develops over time with dedication and consistency. Regardless of where you are with your drinking, drawing closer to God is the straightest path toward overcoming.

In a study published in the *Journal of Personality and Social Psychology*, researchers David Newman, John Nezlek, and Todd Thrash found that prayer has a positive effect on depression and anxiety. It increases well-being, buffers stress, and helps people make sense of life events. It can improve emotional management and lower anxiety. This secular data about the power of prayer is rooted in the truth of God's work through humanity. Prayer offers these positive results because we were created for this. When we're infused with the Holy Spirit, good things happen in body, mind, and spirit.

Prayer is not just a request hotline, either. It's a lament channel, a grief group, a praise factory, and a counseling session. We can bring it all to God—with honesty. Remember that he knows it all anyway. Like Jacob, we can wrestle with God, asking him questions, expressing frustration and pleading for help. God's love, compassion, and empathy know no bounds. That's why he came to earth in human form to live among us in our human struggles.

Prayer can feel distinctly powerful when practiced in community, church, and smaller support groups. Jesus tells his disciples, "Where two or three are gathered in my name, there am I among them" (Matthew 18:20). There's something divine about believers coming together in the Spirit. God has given us the tool of prayer to fight beyond the power of our flesh. He calls prayer and Scripture weapons of "warfare" that have "divine power to destroy strongholds" (2 Corinthians 10:3-5).

Our daily habits can act as generators for our prayer life, meaning they're a vital tool of spiritual warfare. Imagine dropping a single match into a forest. By itself, the match is small and unremarkable. But in the right conditions, it can spark a massive wildfire that spreads for miles. In the same way, creating the habit of consistent prayer might seem simple. It might not seem like it will yield major results at first, but over time, it can ignite a powerful transformation in your spiritual life. Prayer redirects your focus, strengthens your relationship with God, and equips you to hear from God and put that supernatural knowledge to good use. Just as one match can set a forest ablaze, one habit, rooted in faith, can create profound change.

In *Prayer*, Tim Keller writes, "A rich, vibrant, consoling, hard-won prayer life is one that good that makes it possible to receive all other kinds of goods rightly and beneficially." He uses the apostle Paul as an example of one who used prayer correctly, saying that he didn't "see prayer as merely a way to get things from God but as a way to get more of God himself."

It may feel counterintuitive, but ritualizing your daily spiritual life may be a good starting point. Strike the match of connection with the Holy Spirit through a short, two-word prayer: "Lord, help." In a split second, you invite him to begin the work on your behalf. A simple, daily prayer practice like this will, at minimum, strengthen your faith and connection with God. You could consider setting a timer or specifying a time each morning to pray for a couple of minutes. You could commit to regular spoken prayer, silent internal prayer, or written prayer. Once you establish a regular rhythm, you can introduce more or lengthier prayer times as you grow.

Prayer forces us to process feelings and situations we might otherwise avoid. It opens a pathway of communication to hear from God, offering access to never-ending new spiritual insights. Often, prayer reminds us of God's promises, because it causes the mind to recall Scripture verses heard long ago. Prayer becomes a source of comfort and strength.

Consider what you naturally turn to in moments of crisis. Maybe you text a friend, call a sibling, google your problem, or scroll through social media. What if you turned to God first? It might not be your instinctual habit, but I can tell you that I've regretted not doing so.

Praying can be hard, because it requires us to face our doubts about what God can and will do for us. Can you think of a time when God answered a prayer? What doors might you open by believing it's possible for him to do that again? It can be terrifying to pray for that kind of peace or freedom. Trusting him is scarier than trusting ourselves sometimes, but it's the safest thing we can do. You can always turn to Scripture for reminders that God is trustworthy. Throughout the Bible, prophets and writers remind the people that God created them, restored them, saved them, and made an unbreakable covenant with them. Those words are no different for you. They are timeless and eternal, "God-breathed" and "useful" so that we "may be thoroughly equipped for every good work" (2 Timothy 3:16-17 NIV).

Do you see yet that this is not a battle against "flesh and blood, but against principalities, against powers, against the rulers of the darkness of this world" (Ephesians 6:12-13 KJV)? Do you see yet why it's been so hard? We're not dealing only with humans here—we're dealing with spiritual attacks.

Now that we know, the question is whether we'll put on this truth and use the tools God's provided. Prayer is a powerful weapon. Use it.

LEAN ON GOD'S WORD

Memorizing Scripture can also be life giving. We may not internalize the full meaning of a particular verse in the moment of memorization, but our brain files it away for when those words will be necessary. Having the Word of God stored in your memory is the ultimate weapon of the Holy Spirit when the spiritual forces of darkness take hold.

Some simple verses to start memorizing include:

- Be still, and know that I am God. (Psalm 46:10)

- Be strong and courageous. Do not be frightened, and do not be dismayed, for the LORD your God is with you wherever you go. (Joshua 1:9)

- Do not be anxious about anything, but in everything by prayer and supplication with thanksgiving let your requests be made known to God. (Philippians 4:6)

- He who began a good work in you will bring it to completion at the day of Jesus Christ. (Philippians 1:6)

- It is the LORD who goes before you. He will be with you; he will not leave you or forsake you. Do not fear or be dismayed. (Deuteronomy 31:8)

- Be strong, and let your heart take courage, all you who wait for the LORD. (Psalm 31:24)

With access to our Creator, we've got what we need. I hear the doubts—that maybe this won't work, or that because you don't really want to quit, it's a lost cause. It's not true. Action begets change even before our heart is in the game.

Here's a vision that really helped me: Satan can essentially hand me a drink and then his work with me is done. He keeps me busy sipping. After that, he can focus on other things, because there is no Holy Spirit work happening in me while I'm drinking. I make it so easy for him to crush everything else God is working on in my life. Remember that the Bible says, "Don't get drunk on wine . . . but be filled with the Holy Spirit" (Ephesians 5:18). This implies that what fills us controls us. The Holy Spirit may not leave us fully, but drunkenness disrupts his active leadership and influence in that moment. You simply cannot be fully filled with the Holy Spirit and drunk on wine at the same time. One will take precedence.

By trusting in God through powerful prayer habits, leaning into his promises in Scripture, and walking through the hardest moments holding his hand, we can change our brains. We've trained and convinced ourselves that we need help from alcohol to get through. But God, in his infinite wisdom, gave us the power to do brain surgery on ourselves through our miraculous minds.

SCRIPTURE AND THE SPIRITUAL BATTLE

In Matthew 4:8-9, Satan promised Jesus "all the kingdoms of the world and their glory" if he would "fall down and worship me." At that time, Satan truly did hold influence over the world's systems—authority that humanity (Adam and Eve) had forfeited through sin. Even with this real offer on the table, Jesus refused to compromise. He chose the harder way—obedience to the Father through his coming death on the cross—to win back what was lost.

This approach applies to our lives, too. It's not that you and I are Jesus, but that he's always with us. So, when Satan tempts us with the lies of alcohol, we can copy Jesus. He replied to the accuser, "Be gone, Satan! For it is written, 'You shall worship the Lord your God and him only shall you serve'" (Matthew 4:10). This line caused the devil to flee, and angels came to minister to Jesus.

Quoting Scripture, silently or aloud, is your greatest power move as a Christian. We're more than "only human" in God's family. Paul tells us that "those sanctified in Christ Jesus" are "called to be saints" (1 Corinthians 1:2). Not only are you a child of God, but you're also a saint. You have access to the full power of the Holy Spirit at any moment in time. When Jesus left earth, he said he was leaving a helper with us; that helper, the Holy Spirit, is still here.

In what other realm could someone like me or you be called an actual saint? Only in the upside-down kingdom of Jesus. We don't have to play by the rules of the world.

An important detail about this story: When Satan tempted Jesus, he was in the middle of a forty-day fast—hungry, tired, anticipating what would come. Even for Jesus, this wasn't easy. Easy isn't the goal. As Abbie Halberstadt says, "Hard is not the same thing as bad."

Research led by Stephen Schoenthaler and Kenneth Blum, published in the *Journal of Reward Deficiency Syndrome*, shows that people with a strong faith and connection to God have better recovery rates, because they are grounded in something greater than themselves. It's why the first step of AA instructs us to admit powerlessness over alcohol. As Christians, we already know this about nearly everything in our lives. Though not everyone who enters AA is a Christian, the program's tenets are taken directly from the Bible, where Jesus says, "Apart from me you can do nothing" (John 15:5).

Jesus also says that he is the Word. Opening the Bible is another power move. Why is it so hard for us to stop the mental spiral and reach for the Bible? I don't know, but I know that it's a struggle for me. Satan will use your spinning thoughts to push you as far away from the Word as possible. He will tell you it's just a book, with static pages written thousands of years ago. That's a lie.

And this is why your Bible needs to be out and accessible in multiple rooms of your house. Drop one in the car, at the office, or wherever you'll see it most often. Opening the Bible may not always feel natural, but it is never a wasted effort—and it often leads to moments of divine revelation.

One of those moments came to me just recently. I've been dealing with a complicated personal issue in our family, and last night, things came to a head. There was sobbing, accusation, regret, fear, indecision, and shame—a storm of heavy emotions terrorizing our home. I felt the weight of darkness and began the spiral. My first instinct was to run away from the conversation, grab my phone, and start scrolling on TikTok. I know it sounds stupid, but TikTok is a numbing balm for the brain, and it was the most effortless action to take.

But I couldn't ignore the Holy Spirit pushing me toward himself. The issue our family was working through was huge, and it wasn't going to disappear while I binge-watched family dance trend videos. I felt frozen in my resistance to the Bible, but began hacking out of the ice block of emotion. I dragged myself to the living room, where my Bible sat on a side table, with a bookmark in the chapter of Isaiah. My brain spun out, and I couldn't retain any words on the page, but I kept hearing a voice say: Keep reading.

So, I took a breath and started over, this time reading the words out loud. In the course of the reading, these verses from Isaiah 52 stood out:

Rise from the dust, O Jerusalem.
   Sit in a place of honor.
Remove the chains of slavery from your neck,
   O captive daughter of Zion . . .
Get out! Get out and leave your captivity,
   where everything you touch is unclean.
Get out of there and purify yourselves,
   you who carry home the sacred objects of the Lord.
   (Isaiah 52:2, 11 NLT)

I knew God was telling me that I didn't need to carry this burden. He was letting me know that he would take it from my hands. I had been captive, enslaved by the fear and compulsion that saturated my situation, obsessed with the powerlessness I had to make it right. Remaining in captivity to these thoughts was toxic, and God said it was imperative to leave so that he could get the glory, not me. That didn't result in the answer I assumed was right, but I'm not privy to his larger plans.

He comforted my heart, lifted my burden, and told me that it was better in his plan. He told me that he would get even more glory this way. That is our God. He can and does redeem all things for the good of those who love him.

STORING SCRIPTURAL CAPITAL

By surrounding ourselves with affirming messages about God's love and strength and grace, we will be more likely to live by the truth. Remember, the law of Moses tells us to "bind" God's law as a "sign on your hand" and "between your eyes" and "write them on the doorposts of your house" (Deuteronomy 6:8-9).

Studies bear out these supernatural effects. Research led by Jill Hamilton and Angelo Moore, published in *Nursing Research*, found that reading the Bible consistently offers guidance, strength, and comfort during stressful life events. Unsurprisingly, it also leads to a more thriving spiritual life with less stagnation.

Also, it's always good to remember some realities about the Bible: According to Wycliffe Bible Translators, one in five people worldwide do not have a translation available to them in their own language. And according to Chandler Peterson, writing for Global Christian Relief, in some Islamic countries, Christians must distribute Bibles underground. Moreover, the Chinese government controls the distribution of Bibles.

Organizations like Wycliffe are working tirelessly to produce Bibles in every language, but they aren't there yet. The Bible is so important that people are going to great lengths to ensure it's available everywhere. The Bible is a *living* Word. Sadly, the American Bible Society's 2022 *State of the Bible* report gives us some harsh news. Only 10 percent of Americans say they read the Bible daily. That means that Christians are reading Scripture very little.

Cracking open the Bible doesn't release fairy dust that immediately dissipates an alcohol craving. It doesn't magically calm your nerves. However, just opening the Word is an act of faith.

Instantly, you are supernaturally open to the work God can accomplish in you.

I know that you know this. Of course, Christians should read the Bible! I also know that opening Scripture can sometimes feel rote and unnatural. But, if you really believe that the Bible holds wisdom and answers for us, then you can't neglect it. Those holy words apply today just as much as they did thousands of years ago. Let's act like we believe them.

It can be especially helpful to store up scriptural "capital" in our minds and hearts to save for a tough moment. This investment is just like investing your money. It's hard to invest your money today, before the dividends pay off fivefold. But in ten years, when you've got so much more than what you put in, you'll be so glad you did it. The same can be said of our spiritual investments. Of course, memorizing a Bible verse is good on day one—but it *really* pays off in the long term, as your mind grows in meaning, memory, and wisdom. Those verses will be there to catch you years later, in the hardest moments, because you've stored them in your heart.

God doesn't always render immediate miracles. Often, he uses Scripture to slowly mold our minds and hearts. What we can know for sure is that God promises his Word is alive. So and when we open that book, we are in his presence. Yes, even if you're reading the driest parts of Leviticus! You can't be in a better place than the Word of God.

Pray with intention. Then open your heart and your Bible, and read until you hear God speak to you. He will. The more you turn to the Word, the more those words of truth will shape your heart. You'll find Scripture strengthening you more in hard moments, and you'll believe God more than the lies in your head.

When we know and imprint God's Word on our hearts, we're gathering spiritual insurance for the moments we need it. If we only ever open a Bible in hard times, it will help—but it'll be even more effective when it's integrated into our daily life.

Psalm 42:7 says, "Deep calls to deep at the roar of your waterfalls; all your breakers and your waves have gone over me." This verse reveals how it can feel when the words of Scripture bloom at the right moments, rising up as protection when we can no longer defend ourselves.

PAUSE & REFLECT

Prayer and Scripture don't magically make alcohol dependence go away—but they both can powerfully help us rely on God.

- When has turning to God in prayer or through Scripture helped you battle temptation or given you clarity?
- What typically makes you resist going to prayer or Scripture when you're struggling?
- Can you start a simple prayer practice this week? Commit to praying for one minute each morning.

TEN

INVITING OTHERS IN

FOR TOO LONG, I didn't use any of the tools and supports available to me—partly because I didn't know what they were. For a long time, I wondered if I had gaslit myself into believing I had a problem. After all, no one had ever pulled me aside to say, "Hey, Ericka, you're drinking too much." Nobody had staged a dramatic intervention.

I practically had to convince my husband I had an issue, which caused me to doubt my own suspicions. But here's what I want you to know: Second-guessing my problem pushed the ball down the road and only made this struggle that much longer. If your drinking bothers you, and you think you would benefit from quitting or cutting back, there's no question that it's worth pursuing.

When I finally started to experiment with sobriety, I needed to draw on so many resources to take action: my church community, friendships, books, prayer, modern medicine, and just using my sound mind. Part of our human nature is this ability to reason, relate, and rationalize. Plugging into our support systems enables us to reach the root of our heart issues. And as you'll remember, our drinking problem is always part of those deep-rooted issues.

When I shared my story, everything shifted. I went from feeling completely isolated in darkness to standing with friends in the half-light. For the first time, I could see a way forward. The path was rocky, slippery, and uncertain, but in the distance, I caught a glimpse of my own personal Promised Land. In fact, the more I invited people in, the brighter the path grew. Even when I stumbled, it no longer felt like the end of the world—because I wasn't walking it alone anymore.

I've always felt that prayer is supernaturally multiplied in church settings and support groups. God created us to thrive and grow with one another, which you can see both in Scripture and in research. In an interview with CNN's Kristen Rogers, the psychology professor Ryan Bremner says, "There are strong associations between religiosity and both health and happiness, but they are only predicted by service attendance." Plus, researchers Peter Boelens and Roy Reeves led a study that found that people were more optimistic when they prayed for one another in a group, compared with a control group (published in the *International Journal of Psychiatry in Medicine*). As I reported in my book *Reason to Return*, those who attend church weekly are also more likely to resist addiction, depression, and anxiety. Interestingly, most studies on the benefits of prayer focus on people praying in groups. This means these findings tell us about the power of intercessory prayer, in which people pray to God on behalf of one another.

Human connection, especially with those who feel your struggle on a visceral level, is invaluable and irreplaceable. For years, I'd scan crowds listening for hints—anything that might reveal another woman struggling with the same problem I faced. But I never found her, because I didn't know where to look. When I finally talked about my drinking with my small group from church and subsequently joined an online support group, I kicked myself for not trying it earlier. Solidarity, relatability, and spiritual support were everything at a time when I felt so alone in my struggle.

In their slide deck "Value of Peers," the Substance Abuse and Mental Health Services Administration cites research that peer support in general raises self-confidence, increases our sense of control and ability to change, raises empowerment scores, reduces rates of hospitalization, and helps decrease substance abuse and depression. If you have never talked with anyone about your drinking habits or concerns, never stepped into an online recovery space, or had an interaction with someone who gets it, you're missing out on so much potential healing.

Plus, sharing relieves the massive amount of pressure that builds emotionally when we deal with things alone. Like a baked potato in the oven, we need spaces of release to prevent a potato (or emotional) explosion. But with just a little release, it stays intact and cooks as it should. Our emotions work the same way—if we bottle everything up, the pressure can become unbearable, and we turn to drinking for relief.

Sharing my story changed my life. I thought it would be humiliating; or, rather, that's what Satan planted in my mind. In reality, it was transformative—*the* catalyst for real, long-term change. For months, the confession had been pressing on my heart, waiting for the right moment to surface. During prayer request time at my weekly Bible study, it felt impossible for me to hold back any longer. Despite my fear, the Holy Spirit urged me forward, marking the moment I could no longer stay silent.

I felt a pre-vulnerability hangover, anticipating my friends reacting with discomfort or judgment. I knew that once I said that I had a drinking problem out loud, that was it. I couldn't take it back. I thought it meant I could never drink again in anyone's presence, which felt scary. I assumed judgments would silently accrue: *She's a hypocrite. Has she neglected her kids? Can I trust her around mine? Should she even be driving? Is she even the person I thought I knew? I'll have to walk on eggshells around her now.*

I was flushed, sweating, and fumbling over my words. My gaze was fixed on my fingers as I shared my prayer request. The effort to speak left me breathless. The room settled into a respectful silence as the group saw that I was about to confess something serious.

"I feel really self-conscious about saying this, but I have an issue with drinking," I blurted out. "It's been something I've wanted to deal with for a long time, but I'm finally just putting it out there and asking other people to pray for me." Well, I couldn't put it back inside now.

All eyes were on me, but they were looks of love and concern. My dear friend and group leader Lauren (who also happens to be a licensed therapist) immediately assured me that sharing was the right thing to do. When I mentioned how weird it felt to tell them this in a church setting, the group members told me that this was exactly the place I should share my struggle.

One person shared that their sister had faced the same challenge. Another admitted they had also wrestled with their relationship with alcohol in the past. We talked about it, my friends prayed over me, and then, just like that, we moved on to someone else's prayer request. It wasn't all about me. And if you choose to share, it won't be all about you either.

That night was a turning point. It showed me that we are all fighting something. Alcohol was part of my burden, but that didn't make me an outsider. I was just a woman dealing with life in one destructive way, while others were dealing with it in their own.

There's another benefit to sharing verbally: In the article "Putting Feelings Into Words," lead researcher Matthew Lieberman shared findings that speaking our feelings out loud can help decrease stress. Why? Because this practice calms the response of the amygdala in our brains, which plays a key role in processing emotions. Don't neglect this powerful and proven way to help yourself as you work through your dependence on alcohol.

FINDING A SUPPORTIVE COMMUNITY

I soon joined an online secular support group with multiple meetings per day. I could show up with my camera and mic off, or even change my name. No one had to know anything about me, but I could preview what it might be like to fully engage. After a few weeks of testing the waters, I became totally immersed. Very quickly, my view of alcohol dependence shifted—because I saw faces just like mine on the screen. I saw moms of small children, doctors, teachers, professors, and college students. Addiction and dysfunction spanned the entire spectrum.

These meetings squashed a million stereotypes and preconceived notions I'd created. You didn't have to be at rock bottom to show up. The only "requirement" was a desire to stop drinking, no matter why. No one was turned away for not being bad enough, that's for sure. We shamelessly exposed our roots to one another in this safe space full of strangers. It was a fast track to progress that I only wish I'd discovered earlier. When we hear someone else bear their darkest secret out loud, we have immediate permission to do the same.

I was fascinated and refreshed by the problems these friendly strangers revealed on a Zoom screen. Abusive ex-partners, brutal divorces, grief over the loss of a young child, recovering from a DUI, family estrangement, childhood sexual abuse, miscarriage, religious trauma, and so much more. As I realized that others were trekking through the wilderness with me, the journey started to feel less arduous.

Some meetings were dedicated entirely to testimonies, where people shared heartbreaking stories and the profound wisdom they had gained through their struggles. In those moments, everyone present listened with deep respect and compassionate understanding, bearing witness to the courage of the person before them. Strangers opened their hearts, selflessly sharing their stories in the hope that their vulnerability might inspire someone else to heal—and find the courage to share their own.

When we find one person who gets it, it's paradigm-shifting. We start thinking, *Oh, maybe I* can *do this*. It's not likely that we'll bump into a strong Christian woman in recovery from alcohol dependence on the street. But those women are out there.

Finding a support group, or even just one person who will show up, is priceless. When another person can hold just a little bit of our pain, it really does lighten the load. When we bear one another's burdens, as we should, the Holy Spirit blesses that effort.

If you're not sure how to get started, pray for God to show you just one safe person to talk to—someone who will meet you with grace, not judgment. Please know that people are usually far more gracious than judgmental, despite what our brains tell us. Consider a friend, pastor, or someone who's dealt with something difficult themselves—and reach out. Even sharing a small part of your experience can bring relief, and will ultimately empower more sharing when the time is right.

When I first started sharing bits and pieces of my journey, I was timid. Months went by before I could share the whole story, but I needed to start somewhere. As Laura McKowen writes in her book *We Are the Luckiest*, "One stranger who understands your experience exactly will do for you what hundreds of close friends and family who don't understand cannot." It's life-changing, mind-altering, perspective-shifting. The gems of insight and wisdom for those practicing or working toward sobriety could fill entire books, but are often spoken in unrecorded sessions of anonymity.

Each time we share, our resistance to growth loses power. Like a boogeyman in the closet, this secret is just a tiny little dude with a big shadow. Open the door and see him for what he is.

A few months into my online meetings, I finally turned my camera on and clicked the "raise hand" icon. When the meeting leader called my name to share, my heart was beating fast. The words rushed out: "This is my first share. I'm really nervous. I just wanted to say hi." That's pretty much all I said, but I had broken the barrier and taken another step toward a better future. The entire Zoom room of people clapped and cheered for my first share. It felt good, even though it was just a few words. That one action had fortified my journey. In that moment, overcoming the shadow that had loomed over my life for so long felt just a bit more within reach.

For two years, I attended those calls almost daily. The deep wisdom of those processing their pain inside a recovery meeting left me feeling like I'd just attended church or paid for the wisdom of a sage. Something deeply spiritual and full of God was happening there.

YOUR STORY IS A MINISTRY

Eventually, I chose to share my story with a larger church group I'm involved in. That's not for everyone, but I knew it was what God was calling me to do. I soon found out why.

A week later, a woman named Anna sent me a Facebook message asking if we could meet. I'd seen her in the group, but never met her. But my public confession had felt like an invitation to her, an outstretched hand when she'd felt utterly alone. God used me to meet her need in that very particular moment.

We met in the early days of the pandemic, so we settled at an outdoor table, sufficiently separated and unmasked. (You can't talk about your deepest struggles with half your faces covered). Within a few minutes, Anna's story was out there: a recent DUI, nightly six-packs of hard soda, and the reality that her own children were keeping tabs on her behavior. Alcohol hadn't been a problem for her until her late thirties, but one day, things changed, and she sought constant escape. Like me, she would hold it together all day until sinking into the temporary euphoria of alcohol's relief.

Because of my testimony, she immediately recognized me as a safe listener. That's the power of sharing.

After Anna and I spoke that week, she wasn't ready to quit drinking. She was still looking for a way to moderate, to hide her pain. Alcohol gave her something she wasn't ready to let go of, yet I could sense she was open to exploring change. This was the first step.

Fictional vampires lose their abilities in the light of day. So, too, do our most significant sources of shame under the light of another's gaze. When we speak our shames and fears out loud, we will inevitably hear someone say "Me, too." We'll realize that we were never beyond repair or hope, that our problem wasn't too bad or impossible to fix.

Can you believe that God truly has something better for you than where you are right now? It might just be 5 percent better—or maybe it's a complete, 100 percent transformation. But freedom is possible. A healthier, holier, more peaceful life awaits when we release the weight of dysfunctional drinking.

We cling so tightly to our worn-out, threadbare security blankets, yet God invites us to consider something far better—a soft, luxurious, oversized comforter he's offering as a replacement. Can you loosen your grip on the old, tattered blanket you've held for so long?

This is your rescue mission, but you have to participate. In her hit song "Rescue," Lauren Daigle sings about God sending out "an army to find you in the middle of the darkest night." The boat's here, but you've got to get in it. God is leading you, empowering you with his strength to do what's necessary to overcome. We need to take action to receive this free gift. We need to say "yes" and begin walking forward amid the storms of life.

PAUSE & REFLECT

- What emotions come to mind when you think about sharing your concerns about alcohol with others?
- Write down at least one person who seems "safe" to talk honestly with.
- How might your story help someone else going through something similar?

ELEVEN

LIFE-GIVING CHOICES

EMILY WALKED INTO THE KITCHEN, hanging her workbag on the stair railing and plopping down at the table with a sigh. Her kids played with friends after school outside, so the house was weirdly quiet. The stress of a long day at work had pinned her brain into a tense headache. She knew where the wine was before she even left the office. She'd already imagined the satisfying pop of the cork.

Between being the primary breadwinner, housecleaner, and CEO of the family schedule, Emily usually feels ready to crack. Mornings consist of waking up grumpy kids and persuading them to get dressed, brush their teeth, and pack their backpacks. Then, it's nine hours at the office and home to clean, make dinner, and help with homework, and that's if no extracurriculars are scheduled that day. Her husband works hard and loves her, but doesn't recognize her need for more help with the kids and home.

This is typical for women with children, even when the men in their life are supportive. According to research from Hannah Apsley and Noel Vest, published in *Drug and Alcohol Dependence*, women frequently cite "gendered responsibilities" like caregiving as a major barrier to seeking treatment. The study also found that women with substance use disorders are more likely than men to feel stigmatized for seeking help.

When her responsibilities come to a close, Emily usually has an hour or less to herself, which she spends in pure anxiety and avoidance mode. On this particular afternoon, she'd made it through much of the day without a drink, but the craving to give in began to surge. It was so intense and overwhelming that she felt nearly powerless to stop herself from pulling out the bottle and robotically unsealing the cap. It felt like being trapped in a dream, standing frozen as a boulder rolled downhill, unstoppable and inevitable. No matter how much she wanted to move, she couldn't—what was coming would happen without her consent.

She remained rooted to her seat, knowing that she could prevent the disaster if she didn't move. She whispered to herself, "Just say no."

An itch that needed scratching screamed out from her insides. The idea of saying no again tomorrow—or for the rest of her life— seemed impossible. She willed herself to leave the wine bottle in the pantry for now, reached instead for a can of Diet Coke. If one small no to alcohol felt this hard, how could she possibly keep it up for longer?

In the beginning, putting down the drink feels monumental— because it is.

It's a decision rooted in physical action, so in those torturous moments of craving, saying "no" can feel like an unbearable weight. The thought of doing it over and over again for a lifetime? Overwhelming. But we won't have to muscle through forever. We just need to take one small moment at a time until we're stronger.

When we look at our whole lives, we see that God equips us day to day and moment to moment. Nothing exemplifies this more than the Israelites' provision of manna in the desert. This bread came from heaven each day, but it went bad if they tried collecting more food than a day's supply. When Moses told them not to keep food for the next day, some Israelites ignored him. When morning came, the extra food was "full of maggots and began to smell" (Exodus 16:20 NIV).

Part of our earthly Christian life is trusting God each day. Many outsized tasks or goals are overwhelming on day one. For example, writing a book is exceptionally daunting. The idea of producing tens of thousands of words inside of coherent, flowing chapters? No wonder so many quit their dream of publishing! But it feels more achievable when broken down into manageable steps: outlining chapters, writing five hundred words a day, or dedicating an hour each morning to writing. Over time, those small daily actions add up to a completed manuscript.

Alternatively, have you ever gotten excited about a new goal or project, only to realize later that you overestimated what you could achieve quickly? Maybe you planned to completely reorganize your home over a weekend, only to barely finish one closet. It's easy to walk into a new project with high expectations only to experience feelings of failure early on, and then quit out of frustration. In either of these scenarios, we must address our mindset issues. The same goes for tackling alcohol.

We just want to be normal when it comes to drinking. We just don't want to have to think about it. People with drinking problems are often envious of "normies," those people who drink (or don't!) without a second thought. These normies couldn't care less whether alcohol is near them or if their friends are drinking. They never drink too much because they just don't want to. They don't think twice about it and forget about it the next day.

You might wish that you could have the drinking habits of a normie—in other words, that instead of quitting alcohol, you could just moderate your drinking. Many people will try this, and most of us have. However, few of us will master moderation without devolving into previous destructive habits. In my experience, it's much easier to let alcohol go completely. Moderation is like keeping an old ex around just in case. It can easily become toxic. Moderating can work for some people, but it's good to be aware of the risks and mental energy it may steal.

TACKLING THE WINE WITCH

How do we get through these awful moments of craving? Working through the list of habits I shared in chapter six is a good start. Replacing the alcoholic drink with a filler like La Croix waters, Poppi sodas, coffee drinks, or tea can psychologically help ease the mind by placebo. It's not alcohol, but it's something to keep your hand and mouth occupied. There are more tasty nonalcoholic drinks than ever. Quitting or cutting back is a great opportunity to splurge a little and explore new flavors. I've included a list of nonalcoholic drinks and brands to try at the end in the appendix. We needn't just grit our teeth and sit silently through a craving. Small changes and tiny treats can make things a little easier.

There are also some sober apps that help you keep track of consecutive nondrinking days. These apps often help you estimate how much money you're saving by not drinking, revealing where you have extra funds to experiment with new hobbies or nonalcoholic drinks.

It's also helpful to mentally rehearse your cravings. Imagine the process of responding with maturity to a triggering moment, and it'll build your confidence in handling the moment when it arises. Consider what it might feel like to pray through an alcohol craving. But don't focus on forever, and don't embrace anticipatory anxiety about what may happen later. There's enough happening in this moment, on this day, to work through.

If it helps, you can give yourself permission to have a drink later. Just focus on persevering in the current moment. Note any emotions or lingering thoughts that pop up. If possible, write your thoughts down and listen for what God may be saying. Allow the experience to happen no matter how temporarily uncomfortable it is.

I know—just let it happen? Sounds crazy. Sounds hard. Sounds terrible. In doing so, however, you'll realize that not drinking won't actually kill you, even though your mind is telling you otherwise. It has to be done so you know you can do it.

I love this quote from Pema Chodron in her book *Start Where You Are*: "If someone comes along and shoots an arrow into your heart, it's fruitless to stand there and yell at the person. It would be much better to turn your attention to the fact that there's an arrow in your heart."

Focus on dislodging the arrow instead of leaving it to fester and infect the rest of the body.

Experience everything. Refuse to judge yourself. It is what it is and you will survive.

BELIEVING BEFORE SEEING

Embracing a role—whether as a mom, runner, or teacher—naturally influences your actions and personal choices.

But this isn't limited to where we are. We can choose roles. We can intentionally shape our mindset to grow into the person we aspire to be. As Christians, this transformation is spiritual, a fulfillment of God's promise to make us "new creations" in Christ (2 Corinthians 5:17). We can confidently walk forward, trusting that God's plan has made all things new.

He can do the same for you. He has never once reneged on a promise to his people. He always comes back, always redeems and always forgives.

Before I'd been sober for long, I started saying it out loud: "I don't drink." It felt like trying on a new outfit. It didn't feel quite feel like mine yet, but I wanted it to. At first, it felt like a lie. I assumed people would notice I was still new to sobriety, but I quickly learned two things. First, they don't know; second, they don't care.

After a slip-up, I could remind myself that my identity was no longer that of a drinker. Claiming this new identity was mentally empowering. That next day, reveling in the fresh mercies of God's grace, I'd pick it back up: "I don't drink." Because on that day, in that moment, it was true. I lived in the present reality of the promises of God.

Consider what identities you already inhabit today. Maybe you're a believer, mother, writer, scientist, wife, reader, runner, or neighbor. We are already called to many meaningful roles, opportunities to root our identities in Christ and be instruments of his glory through them.

Let's add another—that of someone who doesn't drink (or rarely drinks). Try on how it feels. Say it out loud in private.

No one fulfills their roles perfectly. Being a runner doesn't mean winning every marathon. Being a friend, mother, wife, or sister doesn't mean perfection. Similarly, saying "I don't drink" doesn't mean you never will again.

Maybe it's temporary, for now. Let it be a season. Try out this mentality; don't pressure yourself to be the full embodiment of it immediately. But for just a little while, experience what more God has for you. Remember that who we are as Christians is not dependent on perfection. That whole thing where we're saved by grace really comes in handy here, and everywhere else (see Ephesians 2).

Sanctification and character building are lifelong endeavors, and our sinful hearts will only be fully made right in heaven. How can we assess our current habits—good, bad, or neutral—to inject them with meaning or transform them into practices for good?

In his book *The Story of Philosophy*, Will Durant says, "We are what we repeatedly do. Excellence, then, is not an act, but a habit." In other words, our habits become our identity, regardless of what we think we want, believe, or value.

As we previously discussed, many of our decisions are subconscious. We have more control over those subtle, under-the-radar choices than we realize, but creating lasting change requires a fresh mindset, new habits, and consistent effort. Tiny, intentional habits can result in huge, life-altering changes. The entire axis shifts when drinking habits are consciously examined—without self-judgment—by identifying the underlying reasons behind them. When we say we are people who don't drink, we're less likely to drink. After some time, this change actually integrates into the psyche.

WHEN PAIN REVEALS EQUALITY

Even years after taking my last drink, I can still viscerally feel the anticipation and solace of that glass of full-flavored, velvety Cabernet.

Drinking from a sparkling, long-stemmed wine glass always felt sophisticated, masking the primal nature of my need beneath it. I might as well have been chugging out of a paper bag behind a gas station, but I was a middle-class, suburban mom holding a glass, so it looked like your average night of dinner prep.

However, I wasn't any more worthy or virtuous than someone whose struggles had led them down a different path. My circumstances and choices hadn't taken me behind the gas station, but my heart was no different or better than a woman who experienced far worse consequences. In many ways, I was just lucky.

In the past, I've worked in volunteer positions with men and women in the inner city struggling with substance abuse. Some had lost custody of their children, been fired from jobs, spent years in prison, or became homeless. God used my own battle with alcohol to teach me a humbling truth: everyone except God is nothing without him. Jesus said it best: "Healthy people don't need a doctor—sick people do. I have come to call not those who think they are righteous, but those who know they are sinners and need to repent" (Luke 5:31-32 NLT).

We need to repent whether we're living in a sober house or a penthouse. Maybe I was closer to a penthouse in my comfortable suburban life. But all that mattered for Jesus was whether I was dwelling in him as my home.

We all have poor coping mechanisms. Some turn to emotional eating. Others isolate and numb out online. People chew on their nails, pull out their hair, cut themselves, starve themselves, and buy things they can't afford. We will do anything to stave off the feeling of discontent or fear of reality that surfaces with a trigger. Turning to alcohol is just another item in this list.

THE POWER OF POSITIVE TRIGGERS

Triggers aren't always negative. With intention, we build habits that work as positive triggers. Think about the small actions that naturally spark psychologically good results—hugging a child, exercising, spending time with a pet. Maybe it's that morning coffee for energy or a call to a close friend for advice. These positive habits are already working in our favor. The goal is to lean into them, cultivate more, and welcome additional positive triggers that support growth and well-being. As one example, I know that going to a party or a concert with a satiated stomach is essential to my ability to resist drinking. When I'm full, I'm not inclined to drink. Boom—that's a positive trigger!

Positive triggers can be difficult to develop, but it's well worth the effort to implement them. The easiest one for me is movement. No matter how I feel in a given moment, I can know rationally that a workout will alter my mindset for the better. It will spark endorphins and help me claw out of negative spirals. I know because it works every single time. Another positive trigger? Uplifting music. It might be worship music, or a favorite high-tempo classic pop or hip-hop artist. Either way, music is a proven, therapeutic technique that improves mental health. It's compelling because it re-centers the mind away from the trigger. Fascinatingly, researcher Lutz Jäncke reports in "Music, Memory and Emotion" that music memories are stored differently than others. They can create powerful reactions that overpower other stimuli.

To be clear, there are no magic fixes. At times, triggering positive habits feels like breaking out of a heavy shell—numb and emotionless. I often have to take action without excitement, simply trusting that, in the end, it will pay off.

Brainstorm a list of potential positive triggers. Ideas include:

- Allowing yourself little treats like your favorite chocolate
- Going on a Starbucks run
- Pausing from normal responsibilities to read, walk, or call a friend
- Joining an online sobriety meeting, if you can
- Ordering takeout for lunch or dinner
- Scrapping the schedule and doing something else
- Getting a good bear hug from a friend or family member

I recognize we can't always immediately access our positive triggers. Limited time and budget capacity make things more challenging. If you're a parent of small children, there are so many other complexities. But we must remember why we're doing this. Can we *really* not fit a positive action in the schedule? Or spare a little extra cash? If so, that's fine. But be honest. Might committing to a positive trigger relieve some of the pressure on you? If you're seeking to change your relationship with drinking, you may need to shift other priorities as well.

One idea anyone can manage is to keep short, liturgical prayers (such as those we discussed in the previous chapter) on hand. Store them in a folder on your phone, or a notebook you use regularly. A little intention and effort will help you work through a tough moment before it even begins.

THE LONG VIEW

During my journey, I often came back to that pivotal question I mentioned earlier: Do I want to be praying about the ability to overcome alcohol when I'm seventy-five? Do I want to be held captive to a bottle of wine for the next forty years? The thought of a hangover in my grandmotherly years always jolted me back to the reality of this choice to keep drinking. Every day I drank, I perpetuated those chances, and there was no way to escape that. I wasn't twenty-five anymore, young enough to ignore elderly health concerns and believe in a façade of invincibility. For many years, I'd said I'd quit when I was older. Wasn't thirty-seven old enough?

Our emotions around these issues run deep, making it hard to let go of a familiar way of life—even when we know what's best. But here's a reminder: This is the only life we have.

Evaluating your past and plotting your future is wise. Just as a business without a plan is set up for failure, a life without a goal is destined to drift aimlessly. Time without drinking creates strength, but it also dims the memory of our worst moments. Don't forget *why* you wanted to make this change in the first place. "I never want to forget how intense the call to give up alcohol was that morning," wrote one woman in a sobriety group. "The overwhelming fear, anxiety, anger and guilt, pain, inflammation, and death inside of me was too much." She continued, "I knew I needed to stop, but felt like I couldn't, and that scared me . . . what would happen if I didn't take back control?"

Have you ever felt that way? Thousands of women flock to private groups like this one every day. (I've recommended some resources in the appendix, if you're interested in a group.) They dump their messy lives on the table and ask for advice: How do I stop? Why do I do this? When will enough be enough? Why can't I do it for my kids? What made you stick with it? Why hasn't God given me the strength? Raw moments, when we're forced to admit alcohol isn't helping us, drive change. That's when we pick up a book, join a group, or, at the very least, send up a prayer.

Here's another tool when you're trying to say no: Play the tape forward. Go there mentally. Imagine drinking at an upcoming event, playing out the night like a preview. Feel the warmth of the buzz, the comfort of numbness, the escape. Fully embrace what seems appealing in the moment—but don't stop there.

How long before the good part fades? Before reality sets in—bedtime, alarm clocks, work projects, responsibilities? And when it does, how will it feel? The restless sleep, the two o'clock headache, the racing anxiety before dawn. The weight of regret as the sun rises, the familiar anguish of repeating the cycle.

Now, remember this: That suffering is optional. You never have to go through it again.

Consider playing the tape forward to the next week, the next month, the next year, the next five years, and what life might look like. Imagine yourself celebrating one year of being alcohol free, or gradually losing the desire to drink. Imagine using alcohol in a purely optional, healthy way. Just imagine all the possibilities, and reflect on how living in freedom from alcohol's grasp could transform heart, soul, mind and spirit.

PAUSE & REFLECT

- Which idea discussed in this chapter appeals to you? Which could you try putting into practice?
- Make your own list of positive triggers to employ in a tough moment.
- Try playing the tape forward, imagining a night of drinking and fully considering its negative consequences.

TWELVE

GRIEVING THE LOSS

ONE BARRIER TO PUTTING THE DRINK DOWN is the sense of loss that comes with it. We think about the good elements alcohol once seemed to offer. Like most so-called bad things, alcohol isn't entirely negative. This makes grieving its absence complicated. Letting go isn't just about giving up a drink—it can feel like releasing a part of oneself, something deeply woven into the fabric of life for better and for worse.

It's okay to remember the good times for what they were.

At a friend's wedding, I was the quintessential bridesmaid—excited to support her, helping with pre-wedding details, and drinking my fair share of free alcohol. Between the ceremony and the reception, a few of us hopped into the back of a pickup truck, cruising down the road blasting country music. We passed a liquor bottle back and forth, laughing, singing, and having a blast. At the reception, we ate chicken cordon bleu and buttercream-frosted amaretto cake, danced to "Jesse's Girl," and closed the place down at one in the morning. It was so much fun, and I'm okay admitting that alcohol was part of that.

Another time, I spent the day at a countryside Virginia winery sampling cherry-flavored red wines and apricot-tinged white ones. I got a bit tipsy with my girlfriends, but not too much. We laughed so hard and bonded over the trials of young adult life. That will live on as a good day in my files.

Not all of our memories of alcohol are negative, and there is understandable grief that comes with leaving it behind. Alcohol is intertwined with relationships, experiences, and special periods of life. Will things change without it? It's a fair question, but consider that when life stages shift, so too do our experiences of people and events. We don't want to remain stuck to a past version of ourselves. It's like ending a relationship that isn't working any longer. There might still be love, but the relationship is hurting more than helping at this point. That truth is the anchor.

Alcohol once assisted us in trudging through difficult moments, but with the benefit of hindsight, we can see we didn't need it. I leaned on alcohol through some rough years. Now I can see that those years were rough in part *because* of the alcohol. Still, it's a weird mixture of grief and relief. Rather than clinging to nostalgia's illusion, we can fully embrace the present and step into God's perfect plan for us today. Grieving alcohol demonstrates that you're really relinquishing what no longer aligns with your life and faith. It can feel like pruning—a painful, but necessary, process for new growth.

Most people that severely cut back or totally eliminate alcohol from their lives have these feelings. Many a sobriety memoir (and there are lots!) covers the strangely common grief that comes with letting go of alcohol. Even AA's Big Book of the twelve steps discusses this nearly universal sadness. That grief doesn't mean you're doing something wrong—it means you're doing it right! In the process, you reclaim the good and perfect gifts God has given from above (James 1:17) without idolizing the drink.

Those positive moments—joy, friendship, nature, celebration, creativity, and fun—are sourced from God's well of goodness, not a martini recipe. Furthermore, if alcohol made you feel joyfully uninhibited (and regretful later), getting rid of it may help reclaim your natural, unfiltered joy, held captive by an unhealthy dependence on alcohol for too long.

Think of a moment you loved that involved drinking. Now strip away the alcohol. What remains? Was it laughter? Connection? Music? God's creation? A moment of beauty or rest? Then, consider this question: Was alcohol the source of these good things—or simply present?

God was always in the good moments. It's far too easy to credit alcohol with God's goodness. In fact, the best parts of those memories didn't come from the alcohol.

Questions to consider now: What did drinking take away? What is it taking away? Where are the negative trends of the past and present, and what might they be in the future?

God promises to walk with us through the valleys of loss, so cling to that promise right now. It's natural to feel a sense of loss when leaving something behind, even if it's not serving you any longer. Acknowledge those feelings without shame, and remember that missing something doesn't mean that leaving it behind was the wrong choice. Focus on what you've gained by stepping into a life that aligns with God's plan: deeper peace, healthier relationships, and a clear mind to hear his voice.

This moment in time is holy, because you're listening. God sees you and your struggle, and he cares deeply about it. This is hard, good work, as we chip away at years of codependence.

A powerful visual I've saved in my files, titled "The Emotional Muscles of Grief Theory," exhibits how grief can be transformed with time. In the first image, a woman is slumped over, not even yet able to carry the weight of her grief. In the next, she stands a little taller, her posture more resolute. By the third image, she stands even straighter, bearing the weight of her grief with greater assurance. This progression continues until, in the end, she stands tall and confident, holding the weight of her grief with strength and poise. While the grief doesn't vanish or get smaller, she transforms into a strong, capable person who can now carry it well.

We will not crumble under the weight of this grief. We can and will learn to bear it with grace and ease.

As Christians, we have a higher purpose in this endeavor: to glorify God through his call on our lives. How much more can we fulfill that calling without the distraction of alcohol? How much more brain space will open when not planning, prepping, and regretting the drinking? To be clear, we cannot destroy God's plan for our lives or his ultimate vision of goodness for his people. We cannot undo his saving grace, relinquish our salvation, or make him love us less. Period. But it is worth it to experience life in his light.

God tells us that we will hear his voice behind us, saying, "This is the way, walk in it" (Isaiah 30:21). We start where we are and trust his leading. Maybe you've heard the call. Maybe you just sense it's time.

Here's what sobriety taught me:

The joy is not in the wine but in the company.

The fun is not in the beer but in the experience.

The laughter is not in the martini but in the conversation.

PAUSE & REFLECT

- Can you name some positive memories associated with alcohol? What part of alcohol will you grieve?
- Now, write down your reasons for wanting to change your relationship with alcohol.
- What's one new realization or thought you've had reading this chapter?

THIRTEEN

GETTING BACK UP AGAIN

TEMPTATION, FAILURE, RELAPSE, DISAPPOINTMENT in yourself: It's not a matter of *if* these things happen, but *when*. The Christian life is in a constant state of sanctification. And both the Christian life and the path to sobriety are not about achieving perfection, but about continually returning to God in our failures and seeking transformation through community, grace, and perseverance.

Hebrews 10:14 says that "by a single offering he has perfected for all time those who are being sanctified." Notice the present tense of those last two words. We're "being sanctified" until heaven comes down—and that means we'll keep failing and learning. When you "fail," which could mean drinking, hiding, or even having a bad attitude, you'll always have an opportunity to try again. I've mentioned this before, but it bears repeating: At the end of an AA meeting, participants join hands, say the sinner's prayer, and repeat the words of millions at meetings around the world for nearly a century: "Keep coming back. It works if you work it."

We don't repeat this line just out of tradition. We say it because the secret of sobriety lies in a consistent, enduring, hopeful return to God and group again and again. We come back when we manage not to drink. We come back when we do. I've seen many women return to meetings after falling down. After a few days back to drinking, they came to the same realization: Getting back up is way better than staying knocked down.

That may be secular language, but it's ultimately grounded in biblical truth. When James instructs believers to "confess your sins to each other and pray for one another, that you may be healed," it's another present tense command (James 5:16). Keep doing it. It's not one and done. We will always have to rely on Jesus for help, forgiveness, strength, and faith while we're here on earth.

WE FALL DOWN, WE GET UP

Laura was blind, living alone in her apartment in New Jersey, trying not to relapse and coming back every day with the brutal honesty of a nearly hopeless middle-aged woman. Charity was a twenty-four-year-old mother of three dealing with toxic in-laws and living in near poverty. She always showed up with a baby on her hip and a toddler pawing at her in the background, usually ending in tears as she shared. I hope she's doing okay these days. Janet called in only when her husband was out of town. They'd been married thirty-five years, the kids were gone, and she'd been verbally abused the whole time. She wanted to leave, but she was terrified because she had no money. Every day, she'd ask for a little more courage to take the step she knew she needed to take, the reason she'd been drinking all these years in the first place. I'm not sure if she ever left, but I hope she did.

Each of these women, and plenty of others, returned to meetings after relapsing. They didn't quit coming to meetings, because they realized that leaving sobriety behind was worse. We can be warriors in this way, looking to God's own unending forgiveness and eternal redemption as an example for ourselves. There is no condemnation in Christ, no matter how many times we mess up.

Falling down in this endeavor toward sobriety is inevitable. (And those failures might entail drinking, or they might entail emotionally spiraling through the pain.) But things don't get easier by giving up. They get harder, until you hit another rock bottom. It's only a matter of how fast you can recover and get back on track.

It's why a wealthy celebrity goes to sit in a church basement with a middle-class teacher or struggling truck driver. Money can't save you. It's part of why so many celebrities have addiction issues—because they realize that once they have everything they've ever wanted, it's still not enough. Addiction levels the playing field.

Think of Peter's relationship with Jesus. He claimed to be loyal to Jesus, but he denied Jesus three times, out of fear for his own life and comfort (Luke 22:54-62). But his failure wasn't the end of the story. After the resurrection, Jesus restored Peter, reaffirming his calling and instructing him to "feed my sheep" (John 21:15-19). It wasn't the last time Peter would fail, I'm sure, but Jesus showed him that failure didn't have to end his work for the kingdom.

Peter's story tells us that failure is inevitable, but it's not defining. We will stumble, but God's grace allows us to get back up, learn, and continue forward in faith. Revert your eyes back to the reason you're here.

GET COMFORTABLE WITH BEING UNCOMFORTABLE

Some concepts in this chapter are challenging. But we can't let challenge get in the way. I love one scene from the hit TV show

The Marvelous Mrs. Maisel, where actress Rachel Brosnahan gives this monologue from stage:

> I want a big life, I want to experience everything. I want to break every single rule there is. They say ambition is an unattractive trait in a woman. Maybe . . . but do you know what's really unattractive? Waiting around for something to happen. Staring out the window thinking the life you should be living is out there somewhere, but not being willing to open the door to go out there and get it even if someone tells you you can't.

This scene resonates with me so much because alcohol severely minimized my life. Instead of experiencing "everything," I experienced only broken pieces—fragments now dimmed in my memory. Things felt hyper-real in alcohol-drenched moments, but now it's all a grainy film that skips and scratches. I became so focused on choosing only what felt safe, stifling my curiosity and sanitizing reality, that when I finally encountered something real, it made me sick. I wanted so much, but ambition felt unattainable, buried under the weight of fear that I couldn't be who I wanted to be. In the half-light of a hangover, I poisoned myself with alcohol again and again, afraid to believe in myself without it.

But there's power in realizing *we've* done the damage all along. If we can put on the weight, swallow the poison, step into the chaos, then we can also rid ourselves of it.

Slowly, piece by piece, I began to undo the harm. Not more waiting. I didn't just *want* a big life—I finally permitted myself to *pursue* it in the glorious, imperfect light of sobriety. The pain hits hard, but the joy is much bolder. Wisdom and fulfillment come only through pain. We want a big life—one where we make choices based on the clarity of sobriety and a healthy mind, rather than the desperation of scarcity.

We give ourselves such little credit. We give God even less so. There's nothing he can't do. And there's nothing you can't do with him at your side.

Battling alcohol is hard whether we're drinking or not. But we can ask ourselves: Which struggle leads to a better outcome? Which struggle honors God and moves us forward?

GETTING BACK UP

In March of 2020, the world closed to public gatherings, and our hearts opened to existential questions about life, purpose, and faith. We had no choice in the matter. We lost loved ones to masked and sterilized hospital rooms, screens, and graves. Families splintered due to conflicting beliefs about Covid-19 and other political and cultural issues. Churches were online. Teenagers were in their bedrooms. Women, especially moms, were drinking delivery wine by the batch.

Christians split over their stance on opening churches, wearing masks, and gathering with others in small or large groups. We were trapped, bored, and consumed by the news, our own opinions and self-loathing; everything amplified to the extremes given the state of the world. For those who relied on recovery meetings like AA, overcoming addiction suddenly felt more complicated than ever.

I gave my testimony about overcoming alcohol at church on a Sunday three days before the president infamously announced a national shutdown of "two weeks to slow the spread." Weeks later,

I found myself alone in that same dark, cold basement, staring at a refrigerator full of beer and four-packs of strawberry lemonade hard seltzers. I was back in my parents' basement, where I drank the vodka years before.

When I quit drinking, my parents' house was one of the most difficult places for me to be. So, when I went to the basement seeking a Diet Coke and found hard seltzer and beer, resistance felt futile. No one would know, right? It was fine. I would just have half a drink, I reasoned. Everyone knew I had quit drinking, including my whole church, so I couldn't go back for real. Wouldn't that deter from God's great story in my life? How could I mess *that* up?

I didn't have much time before someone else came downstairs, so I grabbed a hard seltzer from the brand Truly, cracked open the tab with a satisfying pop, and unceremoniously poured the carbonated sweetness down my throat. Let's be real: I chugged it as fast as possible and then buried the can beneath a stash of crumpled papers in the trash bin.

A familiar warmth streamed through my body. My heart beat quickly from the combination of secrecy and invigoration. I ran upstairs to the bathroom, drank water, and brushed my teeth to erase the smell, recognizing the bubbly feeling of buzz coursing through my brain and body. Immediately, my spirits rose, and I settled into the fun—and temporary—feeling of happiness I had missed for so long. I joined my family outside, watching my kids ride tricycles and scooters in the driveway and settling down into a chair to watch the sunset.

I told myself that drink was it. There wouldn't be any more. There *couldn't* be any more drinks now that I had people relying on my sobriety as a Christian witness. But the more pressure I applied to myself and the longer Covid-19 went on, the more I found justifications to drink in the culture. I felt myself reverting to old habits.

Our neighborhood had a few socially distanced cul-de-sac gatherings where, as you might guess, the main event was drinking. I didn't partake at first, but as spring faded into summer, it got harder to resist the nostalgia of salty margaritas on taco night and vodka-Cokes on the porch to relax at night.

At one of these gatherings one afternoon, my husband took our daughter back to the house for something and said, "Hold this for a minute," leaving me with half a glass of rum and coke. It was too easy. The temptation to take a sip rose, and I had gulped half the drink down before I knew it. My mind keyed up: it's over now—now, you're *really* drinking. This wasn't just a slip-up. I was no longer sober. At first, it brought relief. I went ahead and grabbed my own drink to sip on.

Around that time, a sober friend texted me recommending a brand of nonalcoholic drinks she'd found. I was sure she could feel my lack of sobriety through her iPhone when I responded, "Thanks!" I was a fraud. I couldn't *tell* her I was drinking again, could I? What would she think of me? What would my church friends think of me? But, how could I hide this forever?

I had walked full force, and fully sober, right into a pandemic-fueled relapse, along with many others. In a study published in *Drug and Alcohol Dependence*, researchers Amanda Roberts and Jim Rogers found that there was "an increased need for treatment for alcohol and other substance use-related problems during the pandemic." They also reported that alcohol-related deaths substantially increased in both 2020 and 2021.

My plan was to keep it quiet. What if someone from church saw me drinking? Shouldn't be a problem, I thought, because church was *closed*, and no one went out to eat anymore. Sequestered behind locked doors and fenced-in yards, accountability was obsolete. Instead of talking about my use of alcohol again, I hid it to avoid judgment. We know by now that shame thrives in secrecy, sin grows in darkness, and Satan works in isolation. Check, check, check.

How do you handle embarrassment and disappointment in yourself if you start drinking again after telling people you quit? It's no different from announcing you plan to eat more healthy food or exercise more, and then don't fully commit. First, remember it happens to everyone in one way or another—including some of our biblical heroes. In 1 Kings 19, after a great victory, Elijah became overwhelmed and wanted to give up. God met him in his despair—not with condemnation, but with rest, nourishment, and encouragement.

Relapse and disappointment are signs to connect with others and return to God. Seek rest, community, Scripture, and God's strength. Failure never disqualifies us from God's love or purpose. It's easy to imagine yourself failing, and to convince yourself it's safer not to try at all, than to risk the humiliation of ruining your reputation or being seen as a hypocrite.

For many years, I used my fear of failure as a justification to stop trying. Research led by Robert Kitzinger and Jennifer Gardner, published in *Substance Abuse*, shows that 40 to 60 percent of people who try to quit drinking or using drugs relapse. So

I resigned myself to being one of them—I figured that if I gave up my question for sobriety after six months, how could I trust myself not to fall down again?

God didn't let me believe that for too long. The day we accept Jesus, we became a new creation, empowered by the Holy Spirit and washed clean every day by his blood. He's not disappointed in us. He's not surprised by us. He's not going to hold back his goodness. He forgives us seventy-seven times, just as Jesus instructed Peter to do (Matthew 18:22). That goes for everyone, even you.

"As far as the east is from the west, so far does he remove our transgressions from us" (Psalm 103:12). That's the gospel truth at the heart of everything else we do. It's true if you're ten years sober or just one day.

IT'S NOT ABOUT THE DAYS

One of my support group meeting leaders suggested an alternative way to view one's "day count" (the number of days sober). For some, focusing on day counts can feel restricting or lead to an unhealthy obsession, making slip-ups feel like complete failures. Rather than focus on how many days in a row one has, the leader suggested we look at our days as data points. If we look at the last thirty days and twenty-five of them were alcohol free, but five weren't—is that a failure or a success? If you're used to drinking daily, that's undoubtedly success. Suddenly, your slip-ups become bragging rights. Shift perspectives and the light streams in.

Instead of berating ourselves for messing up, we can rationally assess the days we drank and dig into what was behind that choice. What was I feeling? What was happening that day? Did

I get enough sleep? Did something happen at work? Did I experience conflict with someone I care about? Did I fuel my body well that day?

We can't fix a car's heater without going to the mechanic and peeking under the hood. We can't fix faulty drinking triggers without examining them. When we investigate, we illuminate. That clarity helps us better prepare for the next challenge and adjust our choices when faced with temptation. Remember, this isn't about willpower. It's about harnessing the power of the Holy Spirit and, at the same time, editing our lives as he guides us so we can resist Satan's lies.

This fresh perspective was invaluable to me when I started drinking again after being six months sober. It was my greatest fear: What if I can't do it? And this wasn't a private sobriety. I had forced myself to be vocal about it out of necessity. Remember, I never would have made it to six months without telling my small group and church friends. I'll never forget that circle of faces around my friend's couch—my feet tucked beneath me, a pillow clutched in my lap—as I finally spoke the scariest truth I could manage. At first, I couldn't bring myself to meet anyone's eyes, unsure of what might happen next. I stepped out in what little faith I had. It was the right thing to bet on.

Later, when I'd taken it a step further by sharing my testimony of overcoming with the entire church, the pressure was really on. I knew when I agreed to share that a relapse was entirely possible. At first, it stopped me from moving forward. If I could fail in the future, wouldn't it be humiliating? Wouldn't it make a mockery of God's healing in my life?

It's laughable to me now that I thought I could somehow ruin God's reputation. I had obeyed, had shared the truth of what God had done in my life. So there I was, a relapsed failure ready to restart. With a fresh mindset, I began . . . *again.*

Mentioning it to my Christian friends felt vulnerable, so building that courage took time. Luckily, my husband and best friend could both be there for me immediately. I couldn't hide the truth from them; they were both extremely supportive. Over these many years, neither has ever made me feel pressured, or been down on me when I screwed up. They are both cornerstones of support for me; I know they will be there regardless of what I do. If you can find *those* people in your life, hold on to them tightly.

This time around, I knew there was no point in keeping it to myself. What else can I do, I thought, except for mess up and fess up? We're not trying to fail, but we know it will happen. And when it does, the only rational choice is to accept it and try again. Most people battle their issues internally, and they're amazed by your bravery in saying the quiet part out loud.

After a couple of months of renewed sobriety, I opened up to my small group again, wrote about my relapse online, and began processing the lessons it taught me more openly. Today, many of my church friends know about that relapse. Not one criticism have I received.

To start again is the thing we *all* want the courage to do. To do so *is* a real accomplishment. Accept and appreciate each step.

LIFELONG BEGINNERS

Building strength and stamina is a process, and it's always toughest at the start. Awakening muscles and charting dormant pathways is a strain. Giving up will sound like a great option—expect it! If it were easy, we wouldn't be looking for assistance. I don't want to give you the wrong impression: this is challenging. It's long-term challenging. But when we walk into something with the facts at hand, we're prepared to handle it.

If I know I'm running a marathon, I pace myself and push through the tough miles. But if I thought it was a 5K and found out mid-race it was actually a marathon, I'd be far less likely to finish. Similarly, ultra-marathoners (running over fifty miles) rarely run alone. There are pacers, support teams with snacks, water, fresh socks, and clothes. Some runners take short naps, walk for miles, and stop to recalibrate and mentally refresh.

You'll need mental preparation and a variety of training, tools, and planning. Mindset is everything. A quote attributed to Confucius says it well: "It doesn't matter how slowly you go, only that you do not stop." Heed this advice. This isn't about how quickly you can quit drinking. It's about sticking with it for the long haul, and you can expect to get cramps. You'll need water, stretch breaks, and prayers for strength.

The Bible instructs us to "run in such a way as to get the prize" (1 Corinthians 9:24 NIV). If you plan on completing this race well, you have to run in such a way that you can keep going when the going gets tough, getting up again and again when you fall.

Remember, this is not about never messing up. Rather, it's about never *giving* up.

TAKE HEART

We already know that "in this world you will have trouble," because Jesus told us so. "But," he went on, "Take heart! I have overcome the world" (John 16:33 NIV).

I love how Dr. Lee Warren puts it in *I've Seen the End of You:* "Faith isn't a belief that God will spare you from problems. It is a belief that he's still God and will carry you through those problems."

And he will.

PAUSE & REFLECT

- How can you shift your mindset from perfection to progress when it comes to drinking?
- What is one small win you've experienced through curiosity about sobriety so far?
- If you fear you can't live out your desire to quit drinking, what has this chapter taught you about attempting it anyway?

FOURTEEN

SEE AND BE SEEN

IN HIS BOOK, *Surprised by Hope*, theologian N. T. Wright writes about our how our eternal lives begin the moment we accept Christ. In other words, who we are today is a glimpse of who we will be forever. When we live in the light of this truth, we bring a piece of heaven to earth. Trusting in God's promise of something greater than this moment helps us live with eternal perspective— and that shift can change everything.

It's great that we can invite heaven in by trusting God's promises, *but what does that actually mean*? What's the practical action to live through the struggles, temptations and trials?

We can believe something without fully understanding it, which is how we walk forward in the faith that God means what he says.

God says: "I created you for a purpose."

"For we are God's handiwork, created in Christ Jesus to do good works, which God prepared in advance for us to do" (Ephesians 2:10 NIV).

God says: "You are beloved."

"We are children of God" (Romans 8:16).

God says: "I will make a way."

"See, I am doing a new thing! Now it springs up; do you not perceive it? I am making a way in the wilderness and streams in the wasteland" (Isaiah 43:19).

God says: "Knock and the door will be opened."

"Ask and it will be given to you; seek and you will find; knock and the door will be opened to you" (Matthew 7:7 NIV).

God says: "I have loved you with an everlasting love."

"Long ago the LORD said to Israel: 'I have loved you, my people, with an everlasting love. With unfailing love I have drawn you to myself'" (Jeremiah 31:3 NLT).

God says: "I have plans for you."

"I know the plans that I have for you, declares the LORD. They are plans for peace and not disaster, plans to give you a future filled with hope" (Jeremiah 29:11 GW).

God says: "I am able to do immeasurably more than all you ask or imagine."

"Now to him who is able to do immeasurably more than all we ask or imagine, according to his power that is at work within us, to him be glory in the church and in Christ Jesus throughout all generations, for ever and ever! Amen" (Ephesians 3:20-21 NIV).

God says: "Try me."

"'Test me in this,' says the LORD Almighty, 'and see if I will not throw open the floodgates of heaven and pour out so much blessing that there will not be room enough to store it'" (Malachi 3:10 NIV).

What does *that* blessing look like? We don't know yet, but he's telling us to trust him.

MENTAL PREPARATION

Changing something this big takes persistence, resilience, community, and consistent surrender to God. We can most effectively do this when we authentically believe what Scripture says about him and what he wants for us. Also, God's promise to "keep no record of wrongs" can be a deep comfort (1 Corinthians 13:5 NIV).

The early days are tough—getting through a regular week, a social event, or just thinking of forever without a drink. That's why I encourage you *not* to think in terms of forever. Just focus on today. Maybe that sounds silly, but it's the way millions of people have done it before.

Even cutting back can feel like deprivation. But remember what alcohol does to you. Think of how it wakes us in the night—with a churning stomach, a dry mouth, or a mind full of regret. Despite growing signs that it brings more harm than good, this substance still manages to keep swaying our choices.

The temptation to lean on alcohol as a friend, a stress reliever, or a mood booster is a clear reminder of how easily it can distract us from our deeper purpose. When it's time to lay down an idol the world says is entirely acceptable, the pull of our sinful nature becomes unmistakably loud—a signal that something deeper needs healing.

Know it's *not* just you; resistance and frustration are common. That's why making a change or going sober is such an accomplishment. It takes persistence and resilience.

Those who have crossed into the darker depths of addiction describe alcohol's toll as a "death within"—a slow, insidious unraveling marked by inflammation, dehydration, malnutrition, and the relentless sacrifice of the liver. Alcohol's toll on our bodies—whether it's two glasses of wine or a week of nonstop drinking—is undeniable *because* God designed the body to respond to toxins. Alcohol and its effects loudly tell that story. The life awaiting us on the other side is quieter—like a still, small voice that can only be heard when we finally silence the noise and mental pollution.

The two paths ahead lead to different outcomes. One moves toward life; the other, at best, stifles growth. I ask again—is this a battle you still want to be fighting at fifty-five? Seventy-five? Eighty-five? Addiction can be a lifelong struggle or a temporary challenge. Whether it's letting go of a nightly glass of wine or breaking free from years of binge drinking, both habits create barriers to spiritual growth and the best life available.

What will the middle chapters of your life story say? What about the last ones? That choice is one you can make now.

THE PROTÉGÉ EFFECT

While you walk through all of this, you'll gain strength by supporting those just a little behind you, or in the same spot. This is known as the protégé effect: We learn more effectively ourselves by teaching others. There's a quote attributed to author Robert Heinlein that says, "When one teaches, two learn."

As you step into the role of a supportive friend, you'll be surprised by the wisdom and insight that naturally develops. In a blog post for Growth Engineering, writer Harry Cloke described the protégé effect this way: "Explaining a concept to someone else helps you to develop your own understanding of it. The process of explaining forces you to organize your thoughts, identify gaps in your knowledge and strengthen your grasp of the subject."

Clarity often feels out of reach when we're trapped in our problems. But by viewing someone else's challenges from the outside, we gain insights that can illuminate our own. There's a remarkable shift when we move from student to teacher, even if we're still navigating our own issues. Others can strengthen our self-confidence, helping us recognize just how much we've learned. Plus, it's biblical: "Iron sharpens iron, and one man sharpens another" (Proverbs 27:17).

Being a mentor or encourager brings new meaning and purpose to your journey. It shifts your focus outward, helping you break free from the cycle of self-absorption that often comes with personal struggles. This is why AA encourages newcomers to seek sponsors—trusted guides who can offer support and accountability. Recovery groups readily exchange phone numbers and emails with people they've just met, because no one should have to navigate this path alone.

Teaching or leading can offer deeper insight into the root of your own struggles and equip you with new strategies to overcome those urges. Listening to others' stories broadens perspectives, sparks creative problem-solving, and inspires self-reflection, which can lead to personal breakthroughs. "Let the wise hear and increase in learning, and the one who understands obtain guidance" (Proverbs 1:5). Heed the call to listen, learn, and guide. God will multiply that little bit of strength to help others.

ONE STEP AHEAD

I talked in an earlier chapter about the power of sharing. Here, I'm taking it further by asking you both to share and to lead someone who is a step behind you.

Listening to the experiences of others during this time, especially other Christians who have been there, is one way to gain courage and confidence. Offering advice and wisdom from your outside perspective will help them and you. In Scripture, God says we overcome by "the blood of the Lamb and by the word of their testimony" (Revelation 12:11). God also commands us: "Write the vision; make it plain on tablets, so he may run who reads it" (Habakkuk 2:2). And when Jesus heals a demon-possessed man, he tells the man, "Return to your home, and declare how much God has done for you" (Luke 8:39).

The Holy Spirit moves through others' testimonies. When someone shares their story—when they "write the vision," as Habakkuk says—it strengthens those following them. Every believer is called to declare what God has done. Scripture clearly calls us to commune through hardships. And we know that God uses these meetings of believers to pursue his purposes and bring healing among the saints. When we hear what God did in someone else's life, it starts to feel possible for us too—because it is!

Data gathered by Samantha Lookatch and Alexandra Wimberly, published in *Substance Use & Misuse*, shows that social support and sharing are vital to "sustained recovery." Those with more robust social support networks—both in recovery groups and with friends and family—remain in treatment longer and have better recovery outcomes. They are also less likely to return to drinking or substances. The organization Urban Recovery shares on their blog that the rate of relapse decreases the more sober time someone has. After one year of sobriety, the relapse rate is 50 percent; at five years, it's just 15 percent. Time strengthens, heals, and repositions us for success. Community leads to recovery, which results in more sober time and ultimately long-term recovery. Think of what Jesus told us before his ascension, promising us that we would receive the Holy Spirit and be his witnesses to the ends of the earth (Acts 1:8).

The power of the "Me Too" movement exemplifies this. Once a few people came out to divulge the abuse they'd experienced, others were empowered to do the same. While the phrase became popular to refer to victims of sexual assault, it can be universally applied. "Me Too" shatters isolation, offering a new model for healing. When we meet someone who has faced similar struggles—whether they've overcome or are still navigating them—we instantly feel seen and known.

Their story opens our eyes to possibilities we haven't yet considered, proving that progress and hope *are* within reach. Hearing someone say "I've been there too" creates a bridge of shared humanity. We see then that our pain is not a sign of weakness, but part of a universal story. Addiction, grief, mental health, trauma—these experiences easily convince us that we're uniquely broken. The truth is we're universally broken. We're not some special kind of irreparable. That means we can stop being the exception. Healing comes when we recognize that every one of us is fighting some sort of battle.

We've now covered some substantial ground about how alcohol affects the brain, body, and spiritual life. With a clearer understanding of how alcohol fosters dependence, comfortable ignorance is no longer an option. What that knowledge leads you toward is up to you. It might be establishing new habits and patterns. It might be complete sobriety. However, to be anything other than completely honest about what's best would be a disservice to yourself at this point. You have an opportunity to change the trajectory.

NO ONE SAID IT WOULD BE EASY

Just having this information won't make relinquishing alcohol or significantly changing your drinking habits painless. But you knew that. Yes, this *is* a transformational decision. It'll change you for the better and benefit every part of your life, but your flesh is going to push back—hard. And yet, you'll be hard pressed to find someone whose life got *worse* after leaving alcohol behind. Our struggle for sobriety is like "the resistance" we identified earlier from Steven Pressfield's book *The War of Art*.

Pressfield is writing about creativity, but the idea applies to breakthroughs in addiction or other challenges. He writes: "Resistance is experienced as fear; the degree of fear equates to the strength of Resistance. Therefore the more fear we feel about a specific enterprise, the more certain we can be that that enterprise is important to us and to the growth of our soul." Because the brain prefers the familiar and is wired for efficiency, it will resist even beneficial change.

Breaking through the resistance takes effort—we're literally retraining the brain through a feature called neuroplasticity. In the Harvard Health Blog, Maria Mavrikaki defines neuroplasticity as the "brain's ability to change and adapt in its structural and functional levels in response to experience." And while that's happening, our prefrontal cortex (responsible for logic and decision-making) is battling it out with the limbic system (which controls impulses and cravings) for control, according to Ned Kalin in the *American Journal of Psychiatry*. Interestingly, this mirrors the spiritual battle between the flesh and the spirit. We think we're just making one little choice, but really, we're at war.

There are some psychological remedies to this struggle, such as cognitive behavioral therapy (CBT). This kind of therapy helps retrain thought patterns through mindfulness and other ways to regulate the nervous system. But while medication and thoughtful effort are important tools, we also need to recognize the spiritual battle beneath the surface. What Pressfield calls "the resistance" can sometimes be a mask for the enemy's attempts to derail us. We know that God allows us to be tempted, and we must be more aware of this possibility.

Satan would do anything to stop us from transforming into the sacred, Spirit-powered beings God can make us into. To rephrase Pressfield's quote, the more resistance we feel about quitting our dependence on alcohol, the more certain we can be that quitting is essential to the "growth of our soul." Once we recognize what we're dealing with, we're more equipped to gear up and fight back.

Again, I'm not saying anyone's salvation is at risk here. Jesus saves the lowliest sinner if she will accept him—regardless of how holy her life is or isn't. But a "good enough" life or mediocre existence, spent wondering if things could be better, isn't what he wants for you. I'm guessing it's not what you want either.

Chances are, you're already thinking about alcohol differently than before. Here's the good news: Once you see alcohol for what it is, it loses a lot of power. You see through lies of advertising, culture, and the enemy. Just as seeing a celebrity without makeup or a filter makes them less glamorous, seeing booze for the toxic substance it is destroys the illusion.

Could God "cure" you of the desire to drink or overdrink? Yes, he absolutely could. That sure would be easier, wouldn't it? It doesn't always work that way, and we don't know why. We don't know how God may use our story for a greater purpose, but we can trust the promise that he will. In this earthly life we're running toward the destination of God's kingdom, but it's still (probably) a distance away. So how do we find "better" in the here and now, even when things feel dark?

As a personal example, my husband experienced years of abuse and neglect as a child. God redeemed and healed him, but to this day, the remnants of that trauma remain. Despite those lingering effects, he still clings to the truth of God's promises that he learned only in adulthood. The promise of Christ doesn't make things easier, but it does color them with eternal hope. When we stop relying on ourselves and start giving all glory to him, we—and the control we think we have—become less important.

IT'S NOT MAGIC

There is no formula, Bible verse, meeting, hour of prayer, or strength of faith that will perfectly pave your way to peace with alcohol.

Each person's journey is personal and holistic—just as people actually are. There's no fast track or promise that things will be linear. The path might be two steps forward and one step back; progress may not always be consistent. Please don't let imperfection or setbacks define the entire course. Just know that all progress is helpful. Accept what is, evaluate, process, and keep going.

I'll reiterate that whether you stay in an unhealthy drinking habit or choose a better path, there will be hardships. But we know which pathway leads to life and light. Which hard will it be? When I was drinking, I constantly managed, measured, and moderated my consumption. While not drinking, I still fought many of the same feelings, but I created a better outcome with better choices. I was also able to realize that alcohol was never the real problem. You can't see that in the middle of it, though.

Jesus tells us, "My yoke is easy, and my burden is light" (Matthew 11:28 NIV). As my friend Brenna Blain recently reminded me, "Jesus doesn't say there *won't* be a yoke." But, when we release what's making our burden so heavy—darkness, deception, despair, narcissism—we can take Jesus' easy yoke. Brenna has struggled with, and sometimes still experiences, bipolar disorder, depression, eating disorders, and self-harm. She writes in her book *Can I Say That?* that she believes God can heal us here on earth, but that we also may struggle with our yokes until glory.

Earthly recovery is possible, but be prepared for the next "resistance" the enemy will throw your way—and keep fighting.

REMEMBER THIS

God calls us to remember his past work at every turn. Again and again, he reminds the people of Israel: "I am the LORD your God, who brought you out of Egypt" (Exodus 20:2). Has God ever brought you out of an Egypt before? Do you believe he can bring you out of this one?

The word "remember" appears in the Bible more than 500 times, often as a reflection of God's faithfulness—of *his* remembrance of *us*. He remembers his promises and covenants forever.

Other times, God explicitly instructs his people to remember his mighty works and faithfulness. How could they doubt the God who had parted the seas before their very eyes?

It's easy to trust God in the good moments, but don't get caught up in the emotion of mountaintop days. Those are good, but they don't last. You've got to hold onto the bigger promise—the promise that he will remain through mountains and valleys.

I promised you when you started this book that you would never think about alcohol the same way again—that you might even want to quit drinking (not just want to want to quit drinking.) "Right action depends on, at some point, the integration of deliberative knowledge into action," writes Kent Dunnington in *Addiction and Virtue*. "Deliberative knowledge" is what you've been building while reading this book. I hope you've had the chance to carefully examine the facts about alcohol, reflect on how it fits into your life, weigh different perspectives and evidence, and thoughtfully consider how to make a rational decision about its role.

With this understanding—knowing why you drink, what pulls you back, and how your physical and emotional urges cycle—you'll have the intellectual, medical, and spiritual resources you need to move forward with confidence and a clear plan. If you struggle with dysfunctional drinking, know that you are becoming equipped to tackle things honestly and without confusion. Overcoming this stronghold is not a one-and-done task. Rather, it's the journey of a lifetime, fueled by trust and obedience. As you go, you'll find ever more Spirit-led peace and joy.

PAUSE & REFLECT

- When you consider what it would be like to struggle with alcohol in ten or twenty years, what feelings arise?
- Early in the chapter, I shared some of God's powerful words in Scripture. These verses counter some of our most common thoughts and fears. Which one resonated most with you and why?
- Can you think of a time when helping someone a step behind you in life, in any capacity, helped you learn more and increased your confidence?
- How have the testimonies of others empowered you in the past?

FIFTEEN

STEPPING FORWARD

BY NOW, YOU'VE SPENT SOME TIME reflecting on alcohol. You've considered both your history with it and the emotions that surround it. I hope you've experienced a breakthrough or two, and that you've begun to see through the many lies wrapped around alcohol—the lies from culture, from marketing, and even from your own mind. Lies like the idea that we *need* wine to get through events, feelings, or pain. When we fall prey to these lies, we become overly focused on ourselves—on coping, pleasure, and fun—which makes it difficult to notice or respond to things outside of ourselves.

And it's hard to be attuned to the Holy Spirit's work around us when we drown out God's still, small voice with the thrum of alcohol. By taking small, practical steps like those you've learned here, reflecting on yourself and consistently turning to God, you can make steady, pressure-free changes. Over time, these small shifts help rewire the brain. They can help us reshape our lives to function with less alcohol—or eventually, none at all.

Removing the focus on alcohol, or the compulsion to drink for the wrong reasons, clears the way for improvement in other areas of life: sleep, energy, mental clarity, spiritual growth, productivity, relationships. The better these aspects of life become, the less appealing it is to return to the captivity of alcohol. As one friend put it: "When I was drinking, I would survive off four hours of sleep to stay up and have a good time time—now, I'm neurotic if I think I might get less than eight full hours." When we're no longer relying on greasy food to sober up, cravings for cheese fries diminish. Healthier choices in one area of life lead to healthier choices elsewhere.

As you begin to understand how deeply alcohol impacts the entire body, aspects of health like hydration, vitamins, nutrition, and other wellness tools take on a whole new level of importance. You should see the cabinet full of vitamins, supplements, and healthy skin products I'm obsessed with, now that I'm fully on board with the health of my whole body.

In her book *Uncontrolled Burn*, Brooke Martin writes of the fireweed flower, which blooms only after intense fires have killed off everything in its environment. You'd think that nothing could survive such harsh conditions, but the violent pressure of the fire coaxes that flower into existence.

I think we're all a bit like the fireweed flower. Our battle with alcohol, and with whatever brought us to it, is like a harsh fire to our sensitive hearts. Sometimes it feels like we cannot survive intact through the evils around us. But listen: We're not in charge of what's possible. We're just responsible for doing the next thing we're called to do. We can believe that God makes a way when there seems to be no way. He makes the fireweed flower bloom in the least hospitable environment. Sometimes, our bodies don't feel like a hospitable environment for sobriety. How could something beautiful possibly thrive in our messy, burned-out lives? But that's just it: our lives *will* thrive, because we were made for this.

"Stand firm, then, and do not let yourselves be burdened again by a yoke of slavery," Paul tells us (Galatians 5:1 NIV). We have an invisible, all-powerful presence with us every step of the way, helping to lighten our load. But we do have to *let* God hold it—he won't take it without our asking.

I want to share one more story with you.

Kelly was part of my online support group and showed up every time—even after a weekend when she drank. I didn't think I could have faced the group early in my journey if I'd slipped, but Kelly did. She always came back with honesty, insight, and a renewed sense of strength.

Without the meetings, or a plan to access her resources during the week, Kelly might have returned to overdrinking night after night. She might have stopped trying to walk down her chosen path and devolved into even more destructive choices. But she didn't do that. She showed up. She counted more sober days than drinking days and celebrated herself for the small victories. She committed to the journey, even when she lost her way sometimes.

We all lose our way sometimes. And there's always a way back. I hope these chapters have helped you envision something different for yourself. I hope that you'll never think about alcohol in the same way again. There's no pressure from God to "be good," because you're already saved. Your life is no longer just a day-to-day struggle. It's part of a beautiful, eternal story that we're writing with God.

You can't unknow the reality you've learned of how alcohol works in the body, mind, and spirit. No longer will we be persuaded by culture and fooled by the schemes of the world. The curtain's been pulled back, and the Great Oz is nothing more than a fallen angel who can never defeat the one true God. And since you are a daughter of the Most High, the devil can't defeat you either.

By now, I hope you *want* to drink less, but not because of legalistic standards or because you think you should. I hope you want to quit those old, destructive patterns because you've been positively enlightened by knowledge and truth. Maybe, with the examples of those who've gone before you, you see it's possible to change your habits around alcohol. You've considered life with less alcohol, or none at all, and it's not as terrible as it once seemed. You've traveled to the future, played it forward, and seen how close you are to what you want.

Today, you know more now than you did before about how alcohol affects your brain, body, and relationships. You will never forget what you've learned here.

LEAVING A LEGACY

When I think about what led me to five years of sobriety, and what's enabled me to share this story with you, one concept stands out: legacy.

I think of the generational cycles of addiction and abuse. I think of my husband, whose childhood was ruined because of alcoholism. I think of my mom and dad, both of whom were impacted by the effects of drinking fathers.

I think of the millions of people who have sat in AA meetings in the past century (and millions more in Al-Anon meetings). I think of how most domestic violence incidents involve alcohol, and how most crimes occur when people are under the influence. I think of how many women die every year because of alcohol-related illnesses, how those numbers are going up, and how we're slowly killing ourselves because somebody once told us that we deserve wine to relax and we believed them.

Maybe you opened this book out of curiosity—and now you're closing it with fresh insights and personal revelations about the role alcohol has played in your life.

My prayer is that you leave these pages feeling empowered to see alcohol clearly: not as just a harmless indulgence, but as a potentially addictive substance that can harm the body, mind, and spirit.

I hope you can now take a clear-eyed look at alcohol's impact on individuals and society, free from the distortions of clever marketing and cultural conditioning.

You are free to decide—honestly, thoughtfully—whether your life is better with or without it. You don't have to quit. You don't have to cut back. But you can. And you can do it on your own terms, not because anyone told you to, but because you're free to choose what serves you best. You can be freely sober.

You now have knowledge—and with it, you have power. The stories in these pages are proof that change is possible, that freedom is real, and that your future can look radically different.

You're walking forward with a new lens, walking in the light of truth.

PAUSE & REFLECT

- What are one or two things that you've learned while reading this book?
- What's one change you will make based on what you've read?
- Which tools or resources will you employ to help you make better choices about alcohol in the future?

ACKNOWLEDGMENTS

I WANT TO START BY saying thank you to my church family and small group friends, who enabled me to share my story out loud. Thank you to John and Danielle Freed for first asking me to share, and to Waterline Church for unending love and support.

To my small group girls, who allowed me to first utter this prayer more than five years ago, thank you for listening and loving me in that first vulnerable moment.

To the people who went first and shared their stories online with the world, not knowing how they might be perceived: Laura McKowen's work and the Luckiest Club were pivotal in helping me find space and community in the early days when I attended so many meetings.

To my extended family, who was always supportive of my choice to quit drinking. To the places that allowed me to write about this topic: *Christianity Today, The New York Times,* and *The Wall Street Journal.* Those pieces touched women who needed to read them at that time.

To the women I know that see my writing and social media posts but may never comment. I see you and pray for you, and I know you can do this. To those who've subscribed to my email list and Substack—thank you for your support for this work and the ministry that it is.

To my sober writing community: Caroline, John, Christy, Lee—you've all been so supportive and helpful during this time. Merideth, Arial, and Kristin, you were all there at the start and inspired me with your own pursuits every step of the way.

To Mara Eller, for her fantastic initial edits and feedback. You will not find a better freelance editor, so scoop her up! To Kelli Trujillo, for seeing and believing in this book before anyone else did—and providing such helpful, thoughtful, and encouraging edits from the start. Thank you for your encouragement and belief that God would use this story in a larger way. Thank you, Inter-Varsity Press, for believing this message needed to be heard.

To my husband, who has supported me as a writer for nearly a decade now. For the hours I sneak away to write at coffee shops, and his unending love and belief that God is working through my words.

To my sweet and beautiful Abby and Jacob, who gave me the best reason to stop drinking and taught me how to love in ways I never knew existed. Being your mom is the blessing and privilege of my life.

And to Jesus, my Creator, Redeemer, and Savior. You are working all things together for your purposes. Thank you for the privilege of writing down the revelation, making it plain on tablets so that a runner can carry the correct message to others (Habakkuk 2:2).

To be a scribe for the kingdom is a great honor.

RESOURCES AND TOOLS
FOR YOUR JOURNEY

FOR AN ONGOING AND UPDATED list of tools and resources, download my free toolkit for Christian women found online at **SobrietyCurious.com**.

TOOLS TO AVOID DRINKING

Here are some actions to take and tools to employ when you want to avoid drinking:

Play the tape forward. Give yourself a history lesson. What has happened in the past when you've decided to drink? Conjure up those visceral feelings of guilt, regret, exhaustion, and pain.

What will happen if you drink? What's the next phase in this play that you've acted out over and over? Play it over in your mind, and decide if that's something you really want to participate in. Get out of this moment and consider three hours from now. Consider tomorrow.

The time zone game. Did you know that it's already tomorrow in Australia? From where I sit, there's a sixteen-hour time difference, so let's time travel. If it's seven o'clock on a Tuesday night here in the United States, Australians are already halfway through their Wednesday. You, too, will soon experience Wednesday. Do you want to feel like crap tomorrow afternoon? Pretend it's already tomorrow. Australia has shown you that this feeling or craving you have now will pass, and tomorrow will come—whether you drink or not. Time travel. Avoid the pain that a decision to drink could cause.

The list. Make a list (as long as you can!) of actions you promise to take before giving into a craving or urge to drink. This isn't telling yourself you *can't* drink. In this exercise, you're telling yourself that you *can* drink if you want to—but only after completing the activities list. If you still want to drink after that, permission granted. Most of the time, you won't want to.

Your list could include things like:

- Take five long, deep breaths.
- Step outside for two minutes.
- Drink two full glasses of cold water.
- Dunk your face in a bowl of ice water (and I'm not kidding).
- Go outside and identify one item for each of your five senses.
- Freely write your feelings for one minute.
- Read one chapter of a sobriety memoir or book.
- Read one chapter of the Bible.
- Say one short, genuine prayer inviting God in.

This is my list. You can steal from mine or make your own. I don't care. The key is that you'll still have the freedom to drink after completing your list—if you still want to.

Going through the list will demonstrate that this trigger isn't controlling you. You have autonomy over your urges.

Book on deck. If you're a reader, this one's for you. There are dozens and dozens of sobriety memoirs and self-help books out there. In the early days of my final sobriety attempt, I told myself that if I was reading one of these books at all times, it would help me stay on track. I couldn't read a sobriety memoir and keep drinking. I don't know why it worked, but it worked. I paid no attention to cost; I bought any and every book I wanted. I like to underline and make notes, and then learn everything I can about the author.

I've included a strong list of these books later in this appendix. I had a stack of over fifteen books, because I didn't want to run out. Even though I don't need this tactic anymore, I still buy these memoirs. I just bought seven (used, on Amazon) the other day, because I just don't want to forget why I made this choice. For whatever reason, these books help me.

Strategy sampler. When it comes to social events, we often need a different tactic. These are always scary times, because we fear living through parties and events without alcohol. It's all good, though. We'll develop a plan for this.

When I first got somewhat serious about questioning alcohol's role in my life, I began testing a few tactics. My favorite one was to wait thirty minutes before my first drink at an event. With this time and intentionality, my craving often passed naturally. I could feel the evidence that my initial sense of need would dissipate with time. I would get into a conversation and realize that it was never the drink that made me likable in the first place. Other strategies to pull:

Come prepared with your own drinks. I give you my permission to splurge any amount on the best nonalcoholic beverages—or amazing food—you can find. This gives you something to hold and look forward to.

Get caffeinated. This may not be for everyone, but I like to be energized, so sometimes, I'll purchase an energy drink and a package of sour gummy worms to get hyped up on sugar. This may not be a great long-term strategy, but you can do what you need to do initially.

Enjoy the food. When I was drinking, food was my last concern. If you're not drinking, you can enjoy food at an event. And since you're not buying drinks, you don't have to feel bad about spending money. Plus, when your stomach is satisfied, you'll have less room for other cravings.

Make yourself an offer you can't refuse. I'm not above bribing myself. Try offering yourself a reward if you're able to get through something without a drink. Maybe it's a massage, a day off, or new shoes. Whatever it is, you should be rewarded for your good choices. If you can afford it, go for it.

Give yourself permission to leave. Tell yourself you only have to stay for thirty minutes (or whatever makes sense). Knowing you have an out can be helpful in maintaining good choices.

Don't go. Some events are unavoidable, such as a family member's wedding. However, when you're first learning how to say "no," it's perfectly fine to just not attend events. You don't have to go to a party just because you were invited. In fact, if you feel nervous, I'd recommend not going. It's a great excuse to stay in and watch Netflix.

Meetings, meetings, meetings. There are a variety of online support communities. You can join them quietly, facelessly, and namelessly. There are *daily* meetings packed with people who are doing the same thing you are. Their stories and support will encourage you. Most of these groups host extra meetings on holidays like Christmas or the Fourth of July. They know celebratory events are hard for us! Use the meetings. You might bargain with yourself *not* to drink until after attending the meeting.

Download a sober app. This is a minor step, but it can be helpful. The sober app I used asks you to answer one simple question: "Why do you want to quit drinking?" It saves your answer and displays it on the app whenever you open it. Once you start the "sober clock," the app calculates your sobriety time by the second. It offers other data too, such as how much money you've saved and how many others are on the same day count as you. Remember, some people can get caught up in the obsession with days. If that starts to happen for you, take a break. But for others, day counts can be motivating as you work toward the next milestone in the app.

Think about sober people. Discovering how many people don't drink helped me reprogram my brain. I wouldn't be the only one not drinking if I stopped—that much was clear. I reminded myself that there are athletes, pregnant women, and sober people *not* drinking every minute of every day. There are more people *not* drinking than are drinking!

Previously, I'd built up a myth in my head that everyone is always drinking and having a great time. But that simply isn't true. I looked to celebrities who, incredibly, didn't drink—even at fancy events like the Met Gala and the Oscars. Bradley Cooper has been sober for twenty years. Blake Lively is famously sober. Lana del Rey, Brad Pitt, Rob Lowe, Eva Mendes, and many other actors and musicians are sober. You might not care about celebrity culture, but for me, seeing such glamorous celebrities who have chosen not to drink was empowering.

A LIST OF SUPPORT COMMUNITIES

- Local Celebrate Recovery
- Alcoholics Anonymous
- The Luckiest Club
- Sober Sis
- She Surrenders
- Love Life Sober
- Sober Mom Life
- SMART Recovery
- The Phoenix
- Women for Sobriety
- She Recovers

RESOURCE RECOMMENDATIONS

Books

Annie Grace, *This Naked Mind*
Annie Grace, *The Alcohol Experiment*
Allen Carr, *Quit Drinking*
Kent Dunnington, *Addiction and Virtue*
Christy Osbourne, *Love Life Sober*
Caroline Beidler, *You Are Not Your Trauma*
Dr. Lee Warren, *Hope Is the First Dose*
Deborah and David Beddoe, *The Heart of Recovery*

Memoirs

Laura McKowen, *We Are the Luckiest*
Sarah Hepola, *Blackout*

Mary Karr, *Lit*
Jon Seidl, *Confessions of a Christian Alcoholic*
Elizabeth Vargas, *Between Breaths*
Sherry Hoppen, *Sober Cycle*
Caroline Knapp, *Drinking: A Love Story*
Erica Barnett, *Quitter: A Memoir of Drinking, Relapse, and Recovery*
Sascha Scobolic, *Unwasted: My Lush Sobriety*
Augusten Burroughs, *Dry*
Brennan Manning, *All Is Grace*
David Poses, *The Weight of Air*

Podcasts
But Jesus Drank Wine
The Self-Brain Surgery Podcast with Dr. Lee Warren
The Sober Mom Life
Sober Awkward
Recovery Elevator
A Sober Girl's Guide

My Favorite Nonalcoholic Drink Brands
Curious Elixirs
La Croix
Bubbly
Zevia Sodas
Poppi
Olipop
Spindrift
Athletic Brewing Company
Seedlip
Recess
Zero Proof
Little Saints
Kin Euphorics
Three Spirit

Like this book?

Scan the code to discover more content like this!

Get on IVP's email list to receive special offers, exclusive book news, and thoughtful content from your favorite authors on topics you care about.

ivp | InterVarsity Press